GIANT

RANUNCULUS

The
INDOOR
POTTED
BULB

DECORATIVE CONTAINER GARDENING WITH FLOWERING BULBS

ROB PROCTOR

Photographs by Lauren Springer
and Rob Proctor

with watercolors by the author

FOREWORD BY PANAYOTI KELAIDIS

SIMON & SCHUSTER

New York London Toronto Sydney Tokyo Singapore

For Kate,
high-flying
adored

SIMON & SCHUSTER
Simon & Schuster Building
Rockefeller Center
1230 Avenue of the Americas
New York, NY 10020

Edited by Charles A. de Kay
Designed by Jan Melchior
Typesetting by Cast of Characters, Hillsdale, N.J.
Printed in Singapore

10 9 8 7 6 5 4 3 2 1

Library of Congress Cataloging in Publication Data
Proctor, Rob.
The indoor potted bulb / Rob Proctor ; photographs by Lauren Springer ;
watercolors and supplemental photography by the author ; foreword by Panayoti Kelaidis
p.   cm.
Includes bibliographical references and index.
ISBN 0-671-77951-6
1. Bulbs   2. Plants, Potted.   3. House plants.   4. Indoor gardening.   5. Container gardening.   I.   Title
SB425.P75   1993
635.9'44—dc20   93-6663
CIP

ACKNOWLEDGMENTS

In the course of making this book, we grew hundreds and hundreds of pots of bulbs. When our windowsills were full, Lauren and I asked our friends and neighbors if they didn't have space for "a pot or two." We owe them a debt for growing them, sharing their experiences, and allowing us to photograph the flowers in their homes. In addition, many horticultural institutions allowed us access to their collections and displays. Our special gratitude goes to Tom Peace, without whose expertise and generosity this book would have been vastly more difficult.

OUR THANKS TO:

Mary Ellen Tonsing
Ruth Koch
Angela Overy
Patricia Ebrahimi
Steve Kiely and Mike Gonser
Kent Choiniere and Zachary Cox
Nancy and Jack Riley
Lyn Martin
Paul Gladnue
Tish Hazard
David Malo

Susan Sheridan
Charles Shores
Sue Hoover and Ken Hamblin
Nancy Varney
Longwood Gardens,
    Kennett Square, Pennsylvania
The Philadelphia Flower Show
Pennsylvania Horticultural Society
Wave Hill, Bronx, New York
Denver Botanic Gardens,
    Denver, Colorado

North Carolina Botanical Garden
Stonecrop, Cold Spring, New York
Roger's Gardens,
    Corona del Mar, California
Logee's Greenhouses,
    Danielson, Connecticut
Montrose Nursery,
    Hillsborough, North Carolina
The Botany Greenhouses
    at Duke University,
    Chapel Hill, North Carolina

SPECIAL THANKS TO:

Tom and Diane Peace
Steve Kiely
Ray Daugherty
Kelly Grummons
Robin Preston
Starr Tapp
David Macke
Michael Pavsek
Corinne Levy and Tom Segal
Mary Kay Long and Dennis Unites
Rosalie Isom
Leslie Knill
Lee Raden
Walt Fisher

Solange Gignac and Susan Eubank of
    The Helen Fowler Library,
    Denver Botanic Gardens
Brent Heath, The Daffodil Mart,
    Gloucester, Virginia
Steve Houck and Jung So,
    Accent Gardens, Boulder, Colorado
Betsy Gullan,
    Pennsylvania Horticultural Society
Kay Hall, Happy Canyon Flowers,
    Denver, Colorado
BJ Dyer, Bouquets, Denver, Colorado
Robert Herald, Colvin Randall, and
    Julie Padrutt, Longwood Gardens,
    Kennett Square, Pennsylvania

Marco Polo Stufano, Wave Hill,
    Bronx, New York
Caroline Burgess, Stonecrop,
    Cold Spring, New York
Tovah Martin, Logee's Greenhouses,
    Danielson, Connecticut
Nancy Goodwin and Doug Ruhren,
    Montrose Nursery, Hillsborough,
    North Carolina
Phil Miller and Jeff Level, Roger's
    Gardens, Corona del Mar, California
Keith Funk and Dot Pollack,
    Echter's Greenhouse and Garden
    Center, Arvada, Colorado

CONTENTS

FOREWORD

Most of us have some special encounter that inspires a deep love of bulbs. It could be a trip to England or Holland at the right time of spring, or a patch of ineradicable tulips that give pleasure year in year out with no effort whatsoever.

Every year when I was a child, my father and I would hike through forests and meadows thick in glacier lilies in search of our favorite fishing spot. There was still frost at night in early June; and, by late afternoon the sun melted some of the snow on the northern slopes, raising the level of the stream two or three feet. I noticed, stunned, that a ribbon of yellow glacier lilies was cheerfully blooming several feet under water.

This was long before fastidiousness about collecting plants, and since they seemed to grow by the billions anyway, I became determined to bring glacier lilies home to Boulder. Digging about a foot or two deep, through rocks and gritty loam (exhausting me and badly bending the trowel), finally resulted in a corm. Miraculously, a few corms became established in my garden, where they still bloom after the long, cold Colorado winter, when I always assumed Persephone was deep in Hades.

Bulbous plants are built to take an astonishing range of conditions, from growing and blooming under water to the Mediterranean bulbs that must endure six months of drought every year. The one nearly universal quality they possess is their amazing portability when dormant.

The greatest concentration of bulbous plants occur in dry regions, particularly in the southwestern corners of the five contintents. Virtually all genera of bulbous plants find their greatest concentration in one of these regions—*Babiana* and *Freesia* in southwest Africa; *Cyclamen, Crocus, Narcissus,* and *Scilla* in the Mediterranean basin; *Alstroemeria* and *Hippeastrum* in South America; *Brodiea* and *Calochortus* in California; and a host of kangaroo paws and even orchids in Australia. There are notable exceptions, such as Mariposa lilies found at the treeline in the Rockies; but for every Mariposa lily beyond the Californian floristic province, there are numerous species and varieties to be found within its confines.

There is a center of bulb diversity that remains a mystery for me: called the Irano-Turanian floristic province, it spans from the Caucasus and Asia Minor in the west, across the steppes of Asia, through the Hindu Kush, the Karakorum Mountains, up to 14,000 feet in Tibet and Pamir. In this vast cold steppe region plants are subjected to six months of total dryness and winters of unbelievable severity and duration. This is the treasure trove of the hardiest bulbs for our containers and gardens. Here *Crocus, Iris,* and *Fritillaria*—quite similar to those of coastal Italy and Greece—occur on the very rooftop of the world; tulips find their principal center of distribution; irises occur in their greatest variety.

Unlike Persephone, we need never retreat to Hades. There are bulbs for spring, bulbs for summer, bulbs for autumn, and bulbs for forcing, and bulbs to be grown indoors year-round. Growing bulbs in containers frees the gardener of soil or climate restrictions so we can—with very little effort—grow plants that would not survive in the garden. Simply by simulating conditions of a bulb's native environment in a pot, whole new genera become suddenly accessible. With a few simple steps gardeners in the South can enjoy the blossoms from hardy bulbs, while northern gardeners need never again deprive themselves of tender bulbs from tropical regions.

Rob Proctor offers a wealth of information for gardeners who are just discovering the joys of growing bulbs indoors, and he provides countless intriguing

and imaginative ideas to inspire seasoned professionals. He shows by example how easy it can be to have flowers throughout the year and demonstrates in beautiful photographs how these pretty bloomers can add to any decor. *The Indoor Potted Bulb* will doubtless be a welcome addition to every gardener's library.

Panayoti Kelaidis

NARCISSUS 'GERANIUM', PERSIAN BUTTERCUPS, AND PRIMROSES EVOKE SPRING IN THE DEPTHS OF WINTER.

INTRODUCTION

THE HISTORICAL RESONANCE OF BULBS

Bulbs first entered the home during the Victorian Age. The Victorians were intrigued by all things scientific; botany, in particular, commanded the attention of almost everyone on both sides of the Atlantic.

Plants that were arriving from around the world were prized for their mystery and beauty outdoors and pleasure and study indoors. Flowers were so esteemed that the Victorians went to great lengths to bring the garden indoors, building glass conservatories, elaborate staging areas, and fanciful plant stands. Potted plants became a fixture in the parlor almost overnight. And, as gardeners from any era will attest, they were all the more treasured in winter.

Conditions inside the nineteenth-century home precluded growing many temperamental tropicals indoors, for the parlor of the day was a cold, drafty one. Central heating would not be common for years, but the Victorians were determined. Spring-flowering bulbs with their cast-iron constitutions to withstand temperatures below freezing (as they sometimes did near the window pane after the fire died down at night) fit the bill. Life in a pot on the parlor window was not all that different from life in the spring garden.

The Victorians' love affair with bulbs began with the hyacinth. Easy to grow in a glass of water or later in pots, hyacinths shirked off the chill of a winter night and possessed a marvelous, heady scent, guaranteeing an enduring place in the window. The Victorians experimented with other spring-flowering bulbs indoors with great success, but never found a love more steadfast. The catalogues of the age also touted the latest varieties of tulips, narcissus, crocus, and squills, and by the end of the century every respectable Victorian house was ablaze with vibrant blooms in the winter. The bulbs were potted in autumn, stored and chilled in the root cellar or attic, and coaxed into bloom in the parlor while the winter winds still howled outside.

The fascination with bulbs did not end with the close of the era. Bulbs continued to play an important role into the twentieth century. Bulb merchants increased their fortunes with such novelties as *Chionodoxa*, *Cyrtanthus*, *Phaedranassa*, and *Zantedeschia*. Some are still popular today, others never made a lasting impression.

HEATING UP

The increased use of central heating curtailed the indoor culture of bulbs. Americans liked their new furnaces, and they kept them stoked. Humidity levels dropped, and bulbs no longer thrived as they once had. The increased heat blasted hyacinths and tulips into bloom before their stems could elongate, and their petals shriveled prematurely.

Tastes changed as well. The first fifty years of the twentieth century transformed the American home. Homes became sleek and spotless, devoid of those messy plants. The old-fashioned bulbs no longer complemented the gleaming chrome and miracle fabrics; only little old ladies grew houseplants on their kitchen windowsills. Quickly becoming vestiges of the past, hyacinth glasses were destined for the attic along with the horse-hair sofa.

It took the sixties—a decade not recognized for its horticultural passions—to bring plants back into the house. While I don't suppose we can credit hippies directly for the return of the pots of tulips in the windowsill, the cultural clashes of those turbulent years created new aesthetic values, if not a return to older ones. A renewed appreciation for nature and all things natural lead to an explosion of interest in cultivating plants. Plants were brought indoors—ferns came first

(as they once had for the Victorians)—but a complete reevaluation of indoor horticulture soon followed.

Gardeners began to long for new challenges as well. Success indoors with ficus trees and philodendrons fueled the fires. Just as the Victorians had pursued growing plants as a moral imperative, gardeners came to consider the addition of plants to the home as a symbol of a renewed appreciation of nature and an awakened reverence of the environment. Plants were regarded as good for us—they filter pollution as well as cheering us up—and so a room came to look unfinished without one.

It would take one more event to bring bulbs back with a resounding splash. The energy crisis of 1977 forced Americans to turn down their thermostats. President Jimmy Carter ordered all public buildings to keep thermostats set at a maximum of 65° F. in winter, and many private homes followed suit. Sweaters covered bodies, and quilts covered beds. We began to become accustomed to a home that was slightly less warm. This drop in temperature created the opportunity for the return of indoor bulb culture.

As the practices of another era were relearned they have also been refined. Present day horticulture builds on the legacy of the past. Some technological advances

POPULAR IN THE LAST CENTURY, DOUBLE-FLOWERED HYACINTHS LIKE 'HOLLY-HOCK' ARE COMBINED WITH GERBERA DAISIES, KALANCHOE, IVY, AND CYCLAMEN.

have made things easier in some ways, such as humidifiers and florescent lights, but for the home gardener, our traditions are firmly rooted in the past.

As gardeners we have learned how to make the most of what we have. Bulb merchants carry a tempting

OLD-FASHIONED PAPERWHITE NARCISSUS, *above,* **SCENT THE WINTER AIR. SPRING ARRIVES AHEAD OF SCHEDULE INDOORS WHEN HYACINTHS AND 'TÊTE-À-TÊTE' DAFFODILS,** *left,* **SHARE A BASKET WITH AZALEAS, PRIMROSES, AND HYDRANGEAS. 'LADY KILLER' SNOW CROCUS,** *below,* **ARE DROP-DEAD GORGEOUS.**

selection that no single garden can fully accommodate. Indoors, however, under controlled conditions, we can dabble in winter- and summer-blooming tropicals that would perish outdoors.

The Victorians once learned to grow a single hyacinth to perfume the parlor. The urge still beckons. The potted bulb has returned.

THE POTTED BULB TODAY

I'm always amazed when I travel around the country that more gardeners don't take advantage of pot culture for their favorite bulbs. Their gardens are unsuitable, I'm told: "That's not hardy for us," or "The mice eat them." I can't imagine depriving myself of growing some of the most wondrous members of the floral kingdom due to a minor obstacle. Whatever the reason for not growing a particular bulb—unsuitable soil, temperatures, rodents or pests, too much or too little rainfall—there's one answer: pot it.

Growing potted bulbs is open to every gardener. The possibilites are as wide as the range of bulbs from which to choose. In the endless journey of discovery and delight that is gardening, the road to success with potted bulbs is an exciting one to explore.

Bulbs are hot. Pots of bulbs grace windowsills and dining tables across the country. A new generation is rediscovering the pleasures of growing bulbs both indoors and out. Merchants and horticulturists have responded to new demand with research resulting in new varieties bred for indoor culture. Longwood Gardens, for instance, has an active research and breeding program that will no doubt result in calla lilies and clivias in beautiful new colors and forms for the home gardener.

At the same time, specialty growers, nurseries, and horticultural institutions have scoured the past for old-fashioned species and varieties that had fallen from favor but are now ripe for a comeback. Stocks are carefully selected and propagated. As the fascination with bulbs grows, the marketplace responds. Just a decade ago, it was nearly impossible to find a commercial source for lachenalias, veltheimias, clivias, and a host of other South African beauties, as well as our own North American treasures, such as camassias. It is heartening to find such a renewed interest in growing these formerly obscure beauties.

It's no surprise that specialty catalogues cater to the gardening public's newfound taste for indoor bulbs, and have even recreated and expanded special containers for culture, including glasses for hyacinths, amaryllis, and grape hyacinths and bowls and baskets designed just for paperwhites, crocus, and freesias.

This book begins with an explanation of the plants we call bulbs—including corms, rhizomes, and tuber, as well as true bulbs—and their needs. It details the cultivation of potted bulbs in the home, from selection and planting to blooming and aftercare. Separate chapters highlight both the glorious spring-blooming bulbs coaxed to bloom ahead of schedule (necessary to the mental health of the house-bound gardener in winter) as well as the tender bulbs that actually thrive best indoors for most American gardeners. Ideas for combining different species and displaying pots of bulbs to best advantage in the home will challenge gardeners to look at their indoor bulb garden with a fresh eye. In addition, a list of commercial sources is included to aid the gardener in obtaining them.

The world of bulbs is a large one, and one book cannot cover all facets of growing them in containers. A companion volume, *The Outdoor Potted Bulb*, profiles the bulbs that succeed best in containers outside.

Who knows when the gift of a gloxinia or amaryllis might turn into a lifelong fascination with bulb magic in the windowsill? As each of us faces the challenge of providing a suitable environment for a new plant, one thing is clear. The more we know about a plant, the better we can grow it and the more we appreciate it. Learning where a plant originates is nearly essential in providing it with a suitable home. And while its history may not be as important as getting the bulb to flower, the tales from the past are part of their intrigue. They thread through our horticultural heritage.

Historical anecdotes won't necessarily make anyone a better gardener, but they enhance the pleasure of being a gardener. When my hyacinths waft their sweet scent throughout the house, disguising the stale winter air trapped inside, I'm repeating a very old custom. In spring, the halls of Versailles were lined with potted hyacinths (although they had not yet learned how to

coax them into bloom ahead of schedule) to overcome the smell of a court that relied more on perfume than baths. I have to laugh, knowing that Louis XIV's gilded rooms for all their ostentatious grandeur needed the sweet scent of hyacinths much more than mine.

A NOTE ON THE USE OF NAMES

The scientific names of bulbs are important, no doubt about it. Confusion often reigns, however, as taxonomists and botanists redefine boundaries, shifting species from one genus to another, splitting or renaming a genus, or creating an altogether new one.

In this regard, I have relied on *Hortus Third*, John Bryan's masterful two-volume *Bulbs*, and common sense. There is little point in applying recently determined renamings unless gardeners can use them to find the bulbs at garden centers or in catalogues.

The changes are enough to drive the caring and diligent gardener to an early grave. Take, for example, the unfortunate case of *Scilla campanulata*, which has been shuttled to one genus after another. How does it stay in cultivation at all? Most gardeners would prefer a freeze on name changes, allowing us to get on with the pleasures of cultivating plants without a scorecard.

Although some bulbs are known almost universally by a common name, such as amaryllis, they are listed herein under their correct scientific names. In this case it is *Hippeastrum*, to separate it from the valid, true genus *Amaryllis*, to which the lovely belladonna lily belongs. Nomenclature decisions are fraught with pitfalls.

POTTED SCARLET AMARYLLIS AND LACHENALIA ALOIDES ARE SUNK IN THE SOIL FOR WINTER DISPLAY IN THE CONSERVATORY AT LONGWOOD GARDENS.

CHAPTER ONE

BULB
BASICS

An aura of mystery and enchantment surrounds bulbs. It springs from the myths and legends of the ancient past, and lingers in our own childhood memories as we attempted to make sense of the wonder of nature around us.

As magical as the process may seem, producing a perfect pot of flowering bulbs takes a basic knowledge of their growth habits and needs. Growing them is a simple and satisfying pleasure, as easy as growing them in the garden. The requirements differ only slightly. A microcosm of the garden, each pot must contain or receive all that the bulb's needs—soil, nutrients, water, and light—in order to grow and flower well. By taking advantage of the natural growth cycles and imitating the conditions of the native land of individual species, the gardener works with nature.

Bulbous plants, for the purposes of the indoor container gardener, fall into two broad categories. Spring-flowering bulbs, such as the well-known tulips and crocus, may be gently urged to bloom ahead of schedule indoors. Winter-flowering bulbs, such as white calla lilies and amaryllis, often originate in tropical or subtropical lands of the southern hemisphere; they will flower indoors anywhere that conditions approximate winter in their homelands—the abatement of searing heat and the return of rainfall. In addition, some winter bloomers respond to day length to initiate budding.

SOME BULBS, SUCH AS THOSE OF HYBRID TULIPS, *above*, AND SCILLA SIBERICA, *below*, WEAR PROTECTIVE TUNICS.

THE NATURE OF BULBS

Bulbs have evolved over millions of years, and have adapted in several ways to insure their survival against extremes in weather such as heat, drought, or cold. Usually, the stem or roots are swollen, having evolved to store quantities of food underground. For convenience sake, most gardeners lump all bulbous plants together as "bulbs." This loose grouping includes true bulbs, corms, tubers, and rhizomes. The terminology is simple and important. What's in a name? For starters, the terms reflect the type of adaptation, which often governs the practices that we employ to grow bulbous plants.

THE ROOTSTOCKS OF BULBOUS PLANTS ARE DIVERSE IN SIZE AND SHAPE.

TRUE BULBS

A true bulb has a basal plate at the base of the leaves from which rises two or more fleshy scales. Technically, scales are modified underground leaves. True bulbs often originate in harsh climates, so these firm, fleshy scales are designed to protect the bulbs from adverse conditions. Although not all bulbs experience dormancy, the natural mechanism for surviving unfavorable growing conditions, most of them do. During the summer, tulips, for example, go dormant after the flower has bloomed and the leaves have stored enough food in the bulb itself for the following year. The bulb reawakens in fall, sending out new roots to pump in moisture and nutrients in preparation to bloom again. The bulb may appear dormant during the winter, but it is actually actively waiting for balmy weather to send its leaves above ground.

Tulips and fritillarias are characterized by a few large scales, while bulbs of *Narcissus* and *Allium*, the onion tribe, are composed of many scales tightly packed in rings. An onion-topped hamburger illustrates these concentric rings. (It should be pointed out, however, that daffodil rings are poisonous. A friend of mine stopped her husband just before he added diced paperwhites to the stew.) The scales of lilies are only loosely attached to the basal plate; their arrangement mimics that of the head of an artichoke. (Lily bulbs are

edible and have been a dietary staple in the Orient for thousands of years; I suppose they could be steamed and dipped in butter, but I've yet to be tempted.)

Some true bulbs have developed a protective skin called a tunic. Tulip and daffodil bulbs are clad in these papery, brown coverings. Bulbs such as lilies and fritillaries lack tunics, making them more vulnerable to damage and desiccation during storage and handling.

Differentiating them from the rest of the bulbous plants, each true bulb contains an embryonic flower or flower stem developed during the previous growing season. A cross-section of a tulip, hyacinth, or lily bulb reveals the flower or stem nestled deep in the interior. Like a cake mix that promises perfection with only the addition of water, true bulbs guarantee success (although soil and light should be added to the ingredients) just by following simple instructions.

All but the most careless treatment cannot stop the flower production of a true bulb. They need plenty of soil underneath their basal plates for root development, and the ones with elongated necks usually do best if at least the neck protrudes above the soil surface. Most *Hippeastrum* bulbs, for example, are planted so that half of the bulb is above ground, while *Bowiea* sit almost at the soil surface. Supplementary nutrients are not necessary until the bulbs are flowering and begin to store energy for the next year. Most bulbs go dormant when it gets hot, and are best stored in cool, airy conditions. Depending on time and space, the bulbs may be lifted or stored while still in their pots. Having depleted their own resources as well as the nutrients in that confined space, few of the spring-flowering bulbs will bloom a second year if left in their pots.

With corms, tubers, and rhizomes, good culture is necessary to promote flowering, for they do not contain the pre-formed flower of a true bulb; inside their fleshy rootstocks they are solid. The plants, which spring from buds or shoots, must be grown under the proper conditions to blossom. This may sound daunting, but it is not very difficult. Healthy, plump corms, tubers, and rhizomes need only very basic care—sun, soil, and water in the right amounts—to thrive. It is rare when crocus, iris, or a host of others, fail.

CORMS

Corms are modified stems, usually flattened in shape and usually covered in a tunic. Corms look like bulbs to most gardeners; crocus corms might easily be mistaken for true bulbs.

A corm, however, initiates growth from the top, for it has no basal plate. A corm is a storage warehouse for food; cutting one in half (on purpose or with an errant spade in the garden) shows that it is solid.

The corms of *Crocus*, for example, shrivel as their resources are depleted, to be replaced by new corms,

which grow on top of the old ones. Most corms will replace themselves completely over the course of the season, so they need feeding to accomplish the metamorphosis. Some corms go completely dormant, as true bulbs do, in response to heat and drought or cold. Some even require warmth during dormancy to fulfill their needs for next season's performance, just as others require cold.

TUBERS

A tuber may be either a swollen stem, like that of *Anemone blanda*, or an enlarged root connected to the stem, such as *Gloriosa*, or both, such as in the case of *Cyclamen*. The most recognizable of all tubers is the potato, but tubers vary in size and appearance. They are generally permanent structures without tunics, although a dark "skin" is common.

Growth emanates from one or more "eyes" found at the base of the older stem, and roots may grow from many points on the tuber. Tubers are planted horizontally or nearly so, with at least one growing eye attached to each division. They are often summer structures, native to climates of summer heat and rainfall. They need enough room in the pot for the roots to feed and increase in size, and respond to regular fertilization. Tubers store food and water, and they dessicate during storage in dry environments.

RHIZOMES

Rhizomes are swollen, creeping stems. They may appear above ground, such as those of bearded iris, or below the soil surface, as do those of the age-old favorite lily-of-the-valley.

Roots are produced on the underside, and growth starts at shoots on the ends of the rhizome. Rhizomes must be planted just below soil surface to allow the roots to delve into the soil for nutrients. They also require regular fertilization and division of the rhizomes, discarding old, woody growth.

DWARF BEARDED IRIS GROW FROM RHIZOMES POTTED IN AUTUMN.

THE NITTY GRITTY

Success comes from understanding the structure and needs of each bulb, and growing each species at the right time of the year in the right spot in the right pot. The bulbs of each broad category—hardy and tender share many of the same cutural needs, yet some perform better by altering the regimen slightly or allowing the bulbs to perform on its own peculiar schedule. The plant portraits in Chapters Three and Four pinpoint individual plant particularities and offer tips for success.

No amount of proper care, however, can compensate for inferior quality bulbs. Healthy, plump bulbs repay the gardener many times over for the few more pennies they cost; a bargain bulb rarely is a good deal. The exceptions are the end-of-the-season sales in the fall at gardening centers, where good quality bulbs can be had at fire sale prices. Small nicks and blemishes on bulbs will not affect their performance, but squishy, soft bulbs should be discarded. Sometimes a blue mold appears on bulbs, but it generally does not affect performance either.

Although recent international agreements are a step in the right direction, collecting bulbs in the wild has driven some species to the brink of extinction. Gardeners should make an effort to buy only those guaranteed to have been grown from cultivated stock.

POTTING UP

Light, temperature, fertilization, and water requirements of bulbs vary widely. One constant for almost every species is the need for well-drained soil. Sand, gravel, or perlite is a necessary amendment to most store-bought potting soil. It is difficult to add too much. The most cost-effective way is to buy sacks of "car weights," bags of sand placed in the trunk for ballast, sold by hardware stores in snowy areas to increase traction. The contents add just the right coarseness and grit to a soil mix.

Mix the ingredients in a plastic wastebasket, adding more leaf mold or homemade compost for those bulbs that are used to a richer diet. (Compost, richer in nutrients than peat moss, is a renewable resource, the collection of which, unlike peat moss, does not involve the destruction of the continent's wetlands.) It is extremely helpful to add a little water as the mixture is stirred. Not only will the water cut down on the dust, but pre-moistening will help the soil to absorb moisture quickly when the pots are first watered. All efforts at creating a well-drained soil will be in vain, however, if the pots stand in saucers of water—victims of the overzealous waterer.

A few bulbous plants from rainy homelands are not fussy about drainage, and make good candidates for gardeners who have trouble putting down the watering can. Callas and Amazon lilies (as one might expect) thrive with wet feet, but they are the exceptions to the rule.

One of the most pleasant chores of the fall garden must surely be potting bulbs. I scatter pots, soil, and newspapers (usually an afterthought) around the kitchen and porch. It is not nearly as strenuous as planting them in the ground, nor are the artistic considerations as weighty. I struggle with those concerns when placing bulbs in the ground—judging how they will fit into the larger picture in terms of color, texture, harmony, and all those other lofty ideas—but happily abandon them when potting bulbs.

My only task, at that moment in late September or October, is to find suitable pots and soil. Much too much is made of potting up bulbs. I plant them in soil, usually with their noses at the soil level, and water them. That's really all there is to it.

When I first started growing bulbs in containers, the instructions in books scared the dickens out of me. The procedure seemed to be approached not as a simple gardening chore, but as prelude to brain surgery. It was recommended that the soil and the pots be sterilized; it made me wonder if I should wear rubber gloves and a surgical mask—just to be on the safe side. Bulbs are tough and adaptable. It seemed odd that the same bulbs could grow and bloom in my garden—positively beset with germs and microbes—but they required a sterile environment in a container. I eventually gave up scrubbing and bleaching my pots—I prefer the weathered look of old clay—and now I only scrub them when they become encrusted with built-up fertilizer salts. Nor do I follow the often recomended method of baking my potting soil in the oven; my kitchen is messy enough without that.

In fact, I recycle my potting soil from year to year. More sand, perlite, and commercial soil is added to my own compost-filled mixture. It contains the decayed roots and leaves of the plants that have grown in it for the past decade. In the fall, as I empty the more than a hundred pots of summer-flowering annuals, the soil is remixed and supplemented. If I'm in a big hurry, I pull out the frosted annuals from a suitable pot, fluff up the soil with a trowel, and plant the bulbs.

It is understandable that commercial growers take more pains with cleanliness, as their livelihood depends on the health of their crops of bulbs. Home gardeners should take as many precautions as they deem necessary and reasonable. Soak the clay pots first, so that the sides of the pots will not wick away moisture from the potting soil.

Some bulb fanciers add granular or slow-release fertilizer at potting time, while others purposely do not, opting to feed their bulbs later as they ripen their foliage. A fertile soil should provide enough nutrients for the short time that most bulbs will spend in the pots, but an added boost of a balanced bulb food at planting time never hurts, and it is effective for heavy feeders such as tulips.

Most bulbs, especially the spring bloomers, are planted closely together in pots, much closer than they would be in the garden. Most are, in fact, mercilessly jammed together. The idea is to achieve a full, lush effect. I stuff in as many will fit, with the bulbs almost touching. The bulbs are covered with soil with the tip of the bulb barely protruding from the soil. I bury them an inch deeper since the soil will settle after watering. I prefer bulbs such as hyacinths and tulips to be slightly deeper in the pot for more stability later on when they are blooming. If you plan to have more than one or two containers of bulbs, a label for each pot, marked with the variety and date of planting, is vital.

It is ideal, as many sources state, to water from below by placing pots in a tub. This takes an inordinate amount of time, and I have never met a gardener who, with the autumn winds promising a cold snap at any moment, would not prefer the short cut of using the hose or watering can.

ONE OF THE NEWEST TRENDS AMONG THOSE WHO FANCY AMARYLLIS, PROPERLY KNOWN AS HIPPEASTRUM, IS THE POPULARITY OF SMALLER-FLOWERED VARIETIES LIKE 'SCARLET BABY' THAT ALSO DISPLAY MORE LEAVES WHILE THE BULB IS IN BLOOM; THE EFFECT IS LESS TOP-HEAVY THAN THAT OF THE LARGER HYBRIDS.

CHAPTER TWO

LIVING
WITH
BULBS

Flowers are a part of American life. They have become an integral part of our lives, indoors and out. We send bouquets of them to demonstrate our affections, they decorate our tables and desks, and they're the signatures of special ocassions.

Flowering bulbs are essentially living bouquets, all the more special because we watch their evolution from a seemingly lifeless state to full-blown beauty. They never fail to breathe life into a room. Bulbs fit naturally into any setting, whether it is Shaker spare, deco smooth, or Regency romantic. From the sideboard to the board-room, a pot of bulbs commands attention as well as enhancing the objects with which it is displayed. I sometimes think fireplace mantles were designed for the sole purpose of grouping our favorite things with our favorite flowers. A roaring blaze, however, is hard on living plants perched above.

As gardeners master the art of growing bulbs, they enjoy the challenge of displaying them to best advantage. Containers set the tone. Finding the right one, that complements both the setting and the flowers, is important. Putting individually-grown bulbs together is practicing the art of arranging with live plants. It is easy and rewarding to combine flowering bulbs with foliage plants and annuals for spectacular results. It's all a part of living with bulbs.

AN OLD BLUE WILLOW MUG BECOMES A CACHEPOT FOR MINIATURE CYCLAMEN, *above.* BULB FANCIERS CAN NEVER HAVE TOO MANY TERRA-COTTA POTS, *below.*

CHOOSING A CONTAINER

The simple terra-cotta pot is the time-honored, traditional container for many bulbs. The squat "bulb pan" is the most convenient for spring-bloomers, for it provides enough room for the bulbs to root, and the gardener can judge root development by seeing how many have poked through the drainage hole. Deeper pots are perfectly acceptable for spring-flowering bulbs —and actually beneficial for most *Narcissus* —but make it more difficult to gauge root growth. Some of the larger bulbs also require a deeper pot.

Plastic pots pose no problems, although they must be watered somewhat differently since the sides do not "breath" as clay ones do. They must not be allowed to become water-logged. Gardeners have never embraced plastic pots for reasons of taste as well, but they can be concealed in decorative containers.

Containers without drainage holes should be avoided at planting time. You can always slide a pot that drains well into a pretty ceramic container when it is in its final blooming stage.

Fibrous peat pots have merit for special uses, especially for spring bloomers. For example, it is very difficult to plant different types of bulbs in one container and then coax them to bloom at the same time. With peat pots, however, they may be brought out of winter's chill at various times and combined together in mixed arrangements, by dropping the entire pots into the soil, without disturbing the roots.

MOSS CONCEALS PLASTIC POTS OF GRAPE HYACINTHS, CROCUS, HYACINTHS, CREEPING FIG, AND AFRICAN VIOLETS.

A FINE AFFAIR

Most of us associate certain flowers with special occasions. The Victorians spoke the "language of flowers," and assigned a meaning to every blossom. Theirs was a very complicated dialogue of romance and intrigue; flowers boldly proclaimed the love they were too timid to confess, or whispered the rejection they were too polite to utter aloud.

Times have changed. We say what we feel, perhaps because it is tedious to carry around a book of confusing floral emblem codes—and one cannot always get hold of a spray of wisteria when it is needed. It meant "Welcome, fair stranger," as I recall, although if it was offered with the left hand, after turning around twice during a full moon, the meaning changed to "I believe you are in league with the butcher." Or something to that effect.

The tradition lingers, however, in a less complicated form. A yellow rose still stands for friendship, a red one for true love. Yellow and red tulips imply the same meanings, thanks to the Victorians, who couldn't just drop everything until the roses came into bloom. (Red tulips originally stood for violent love—but I just can't picture Carmen with a red tulip between her teeth, perhaps no one else could either.)

The flowers of many of our favorite bulbs have meanings in the antiquated system, while over the past century others have taken on associations of their own. Any pot of blooming flowers makes a statement of affection or esteem, and some are still especially relevant to special occasions.

For many the Christmas holidays recall memories of the scent of paperwhites intermingled with fragrant pine boughs, and the startling blossoms of the amaryllis, properly *Hippeastrum*. A gift of paperwhites or jonquils meant "I desire a return of affection" to Victorians. The flowers could also be used to tell a suitor to back off: their scent, pleasant at first, was (and is) regarded by some as overpowering and oppresive. An amaryllis stood for pride and haughtiness. In the present day, both have become yuletide symbols almost as important as the tree and poinsettia. Paperwhites, with their snowy white petals and heavenly scent evoke images of angels and starry nights, while regal amaryllis blossoms have come to represent goodwill and the new year.

Other bulbs have been incorporated into the Christmas holidays. Cyclamens, blooming with butterfly-like flowers in the coldest months of the year, convey a sense of hope. The diminutive bulbs of early spring fill the new year with vibrancy and hope. Crocus meant "youthful gladness" in the nineteenth century. That hasn't changed a bit. Pots of crocus make fitting decorations for a bridal shower or dinner, or for a birth or christening. Lily-of-the-valley has traditionally been a bride's favorite, and it makes a pretty gift the couple can later plant in the garden.

A hyacinth stood for sport or play at one time; I suppose one might turn up at a super bowl party with a pot of them (in team colors, of course). The playful part of the old meaning is still very much in vogue, since the presence of pots of hyacinths lends elegance to any party. The scent works wonders at a dance, dinner party, or tea, setting a magical mood.

Lilies stood for majesty, as well they might, and the Madonna lily (*Lilium candidum*) has a long association with the Virgin Mary. It is a twentieth-century phenomenon that its cousin *L. longiflorum* has become the Easter lily. Other flowers vie for a place in the Easter parade, but the lily still towers above them all.

Perhaps time hasn't changed our priorities all that much. Love is still the most important message to send. Daffodils send best regards (yellow has never been the color of *amour* in this language.) Could there be a better present for a friend? Iris, of all things, meant "ardor" and "flame" at one time. This is surprising, considering their current girl next-door image.

A pot of flowering bulbs is a pretty thing to be enjoyed anywhere in the house. The dining or coffee table is a logical choice; so too is a desk or hallway breakfront. A pot of spring blossoms is sometimes best when it comes as a surprise: lily-of-the-valley on a bedside table with books, or glory-of-the-snow perched on a bathroom vanity. A pot of species tulips, clustered among the cannisters, pleases a cook.

Pretty pots of home-grown bulbs, personalized for the recipient, make wonderful gifts. A paint bucket stuffed with brilliant tulips or vibrant *Ranunculus* might congratulate friends on the completion of a remodeling project. Pots of golden daffodils, displayed in an old-fashioned suitcase, serve as the focal point of a bon voyage party. A wine crate, planted with grape hyacinths, adds tongue-in-cheek frivolity to a New Year's celebration.

Living with bulbs throughout the year invites experimentation and creativity. New traditions stem from the joy of growing pots of bulbs and incorporating them into the fabric of our lives. Their flowers enhance special occasions and become recurring motifs throughout the year. Their beauty is seasonal, but the rewards are permanent.

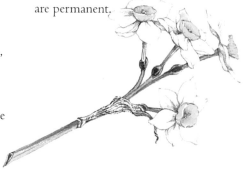

CHAPTER THREE

WINDOWSILL SPLENDOR

Hardy
Spring-flowering
Bulbs

Gardeners have a special affection for the flowers of spring. Each of us remembers our first childhood encounters—the discovery of snowdrops and crocus miraculously blooming in the snow, and later, the incredible budding of tulips and daffodils. I can still recall finding, at the age of six, tulips growing at our new house, and the dusky sweet scent of their mysterious interiors.

Is it any wonder that gardeners devise ways to hurry the season along a bit indoors? The practice of inducing spring-flowering bulbs to bloom in pots on the windowsill is a relatively simple one: there must be a winter before there is a spring.

A period of cold treatment, necessary in the life cycle of these hardy bulbs (but shorter than a true autumn and winter), must be provided. Having evolved in temperate climates, a winter chill is as important to hardy, spring-flowering bulbs as is the spring itself. An artificial spring indoors then simulates the transition of seasons not yet evident in the garden. The gardener cleverly compresses the seasons; having passed from "winter" into "spring," in as little as ten weeks, the bulbs respond to the warm air and light, growing and flowering ahead of schedule. In the past, the process was called forcing. The term has fallen somewhat into disfavor as of late, for it implies more manipulation than simulation.

The gardener simply provides a spring-like environment after the bulbs have endured the autumn and winter cooling treatment that they need to flower. The calendar may say winter, and snow may still blanket the ground, but indoors it's spring. These hardy bulbs grow actively during this entire period, and enter true dormancy only during the summer.

Pots of narcissus and squills on the windowsill are not limited to gardeners who must endure cold winters. Gardeners in southern states and mild, maritime areas may enjoy a bounty of bulbs indoors that they are regularly denied in the garden because their winters are not cold enough. Spring bulbs must be treated like annuals in the gardens of these warm areas, and their blooming period is often cut short by early heat waves. The labor involved—in planting and removing the bulbs—for a few fleeting weeks of flowers tends to discourage even the most enthusiastic of us, no matter how fond of them we may be. Potted bulbs indoors offers an answer to this problem.

Even in temperate climates, where the prerequisite winter is amply provided by nature and bulbs are soundly perennial, many gardeners are hesitant, for aesthetic reasons, to plant some kinds of bulbs in the garden. Plump, stiff hyacinths often look out of place in madcap cottage gardens, informal herbaceous borders, or naturalistic gardens. As adamant as I am about outlawing them from my beds and borders, I can't imagine a winter indoors without them. It's an age-old affection. The thirteenth-century Persian poet, Saadi, held them in high esteem:

> If of thy mortal goods thou art bereft,
> And from thy slender store two loaves
>   alone to thee are left,
> Sell one, and with the dole
> Buy hyacinths to feed thy soul.

Saadi may have been a bit more fanatical than most of us about hyacinths—and a darned good rhymer in thirteenth-century Old Persian—but I am reminded of his words each winter.

Hybrid tulips, for the same reason as hyacinths, don't appeal to many gardeners in garden groupings. Yet indoors our sensibilities change. A pot of tulips, or any other bulb, is essentially a living bouquet. We admire the flowers for their color, form, and scent. What looks out of place to some in the garden will be judged by a different standard indoors, and simply enjoyed for what it is—the glorious floral embodiment of spring—without concern for its placement in a flower bed.

A LIVING BOUQUET OF 'HAPPY FAMILY' TULIPS, 'LADY DERBY' HYACINTHS, AND CINERARIA ARE ACCENTED BY PUSSY WILLOWS ON THE WINTER WINDOWSILL.

THE BIG CHILL

Gardeners pot hardy bulbs (those plants that can survive outdoors in temperate climes) in early fall if they find time, and later if they do not. Finding a wintering place for the newly-potted bulbs is the most important part of the entire procedure. It requires ingenuity and, quite frankly, the first year is always a learning experience. A dark, unheated garage, crawl space, or cellar is the answer for many gardeners. Most basements are too warm. Cold frames can be utilized if the pots are mulched with straw, salt hay, or dry leaves.

Trenches dug in the garden may be used in cold areas, as long as the gardener can determine how deep frost penetrates and place pots below that level. The pots are covered with sand (with several inches underneath for good drainage), then mulched with hay or pine boughs. This will not work where winters are mild, as the bulbs will never be properly chilled. Trenches are also impractical in areas blanked by deep snows, for the aggravation caused by the task of getting to the bulbs overwhelms any desire to do so.

It is entirely possible to forego the trench altogether. The pots can be snuggled closely together and mounded with perlite or sand (soil will freeze and be difficult to dig through later) and mulched heavily. The porous covering allows moisture to penetrate, whether from the skies or the watering can. This mounding process is one of the easiest, and it is as close as it comes to growing the bulbs in the garden itself.

With a mound, it is difficult to keep tabs on root development, and the bulbs must be uncovered before they spurt into growth, because the new shoots are easily snapped off when the covering is removed. Gardeners may also discover that they have built a winter condo for mice, who have moved in and raided the cupboards.

The absolute best place to force bulbs (perhaps with the exception of a cool greenhouse) is in an old refrigerator—the types with the rounded tops. Vintage refrigerators can often be purchased for very little. The advantage they offer is the absence of a frost-free feature. All modern refrigerators seem to have this feature; it sucks the moisture out of the interior to prevent the build-up of ice. (This is why it is possible today, as I have done, to discover a perfect, albeit dessicated, artichoke in the back of the vegetable bin several years after its purchase.) Manufacturers did not have bulb growers in mind when they went frost-free. The old models do not suck the air bone-dry, so they make a more suitable environment for living bulbs. Stashed in the basement or heated garage, the bulbs so interred in a refrigerator can be carefully monitored and the temperature gradually lowered.

This is not to say that modern refrigerators can't be used to chill bulbs, but it requires a bit more work.

Encase pots in plastic bags perforated with very small airholes. Watch for molds and if they occur spray them with a weak solution of liquid Lysol® (one tablespoon added to a gallon of water). It is also wise to avoid storing fruit in the same refrigerator.

In a normal year (if that ever happens anywhere) the temperatures will fall gradually in autumn. Nestled in their protected rooting chamber—be it refrigerator, mound, trench, or garage—the bulbs initiate root growth while it is still relatively warm, at about 45° or 50° F., just as they do in the garden. As the temperature drops, the roots feed the bulb and nourish the embryonic flowers inside. The ideal situation is for the temperature to hover just above freezing for the final month or so. In the real world, the sequence of temperature drops is not critical. If bulb species in the wild depended on temperatures dropping by increments each fall, they'd be extinct.

The length of the cold treatment varies, depending on the type of bulb. Crocus need the least amount of time—about ten weeks—while some allium species require the longest—up to twenty-two weeks. Most tulips and daffodils require twelve to fourteen weeks of winter chill. One gardener's conditions vary so much from another's that timing can only be approximated. The general rule regarding the length of chilling is the longer the better; rushing the process rarely works.

For a comprehensive listing of temperatures and times, refer to the chilling table on page 124.

The pots must be kept moist throughout this period, but not sopping wet or the bulbs may rot. Two signs signal that a pot is ready to be brought inside: the drainage hole of a pot will be clogged with roots, and the bulb initiates top growth. With most bulbs, the leaves should be at least an inch tall before the pot is brought indoors. Pots that are ready can be held back for a few weeks if one wants to stagger the display. The leaves will continue to grow slowly in cold storage, and can be as long as six inches with tulips, for example, and still be grown on successfully when they are taken out.

I am lucky. My unheated garage makes a good cold chamber, although I have to admit its size precludes keeping a car and bulbs in it at the same time. The car loses. A garage, however, is not always perfect, as I discovered one winter when temperatures dipped to record lows for weeks on end. Most spring-flowering bulbs can take temperatures below freezing without suffering harm, but potted bulbs are considerably more vulnerable than those in the garden.

It is possible to provide extra protection during arctic blasts by covering pots with old blankets, cardboard, and newspapers, or even using a small spaceheater. It must be positioned to keep frost out of the area without raising the temperature much above 40° F.

TRANSITIONS

Success or failure is usually based on several factors. Assuming that good, healthy bulbs were planted in the first place, and that they went through a cold treatment at reasonable temperatures for the proper length of time, most gardeners are home free. Almost. The transition from winter to spring is crucial.

Pots of bulbs need a gentle acclimation to increased temperature and light. It is a trauma to be abruptly removed from a cool, dark place and exposed to burning sunlight, as anyone who attends a movie matinee will attest. The transition must be gradual for the pot of bulbs. A cool, north- or east-facing window works just fine. My glass-enclosed back porch, chilly as it seems to humans at 40° or 45° F. at night, makes a perfect transitional area. Some gardeners find similar areas in unheated spare bedrooms or basements with windows. Florescent lights, hung in cool basements, solve the problem for many bulb enthusiasts. Florescent bulbs generate very little heat, and the lights, while not intense enough to burn, provide enough illumination for good leaf and bud development.

Bulb blasting is the result of a bad transition. The plants will send up flower stalks, but they dry up and wither—the buds have "blasted." This is caused by attempting to grow the bulbs where it is too hot, or from lack of water during the whole procedure. Some houses are simply too hot and too dry. These are the flowers of spring, after all, not those of the dog days of summer.

Some adjustments may be made to accommodate them. A window greenhouse is perfectly suited, provided it has a venting system to prevent the build-up of heat on a sunny day. A bay window offers similar possibilities, and is especially effective if the drapes are drawn at night, keeping the bay cooler than the rest of the room.

Night temperature is a key factor in growing bulbs. In the case of almost all of the spring-flowering ones, a night temperature somewhere between 40° and 50° F. is best. It can dip lower, of course, as it does in the garden, but it should not rise much higher. A corresponding rise in day temperatures, by 15° or even 20° F., is acceptable—as it is outdoors—but the less fluctuation, the better. It is best to shoot for the night temperature indoors at which a plant performs best outdoors.

A stocky, healthy plant is produced when temperatures are low and light is bright. Some years are kinder than others. Spindly plants, reaching for the light, speak of too dim a position. Cloudy winters, even in a glass house, produce what are known as "skyscrapers," as the bulbs stretch out more than normal. A relatively inconspicuous "girdle" of stakes and strings encircling the foliage keeps the skyscrapers from tumbling. A girdle is often necessary for tulips, daffodils, and other taller bulbs such as camassias.

Supplemental light, four to six hours each day, can help reduce stretching in window-grown plants. Commercial growers often apply growth-retardant chemicals that inhibit the length of stems and leaves. Most home gardeners eschew this treatment, feeling that a little elongation is preferable to a squat, dumpy look. I side with them.

All bulbs require attentive watering, and frequent doses of a balanced fertilizer, particularly after flowering. The production of their flowers, after all, requires a huge expenditure of energy. Bulbs go right to work after they bloom, storing energy for the next year.

THE CROWNING GLORY

Timing the blooming of bulbs is a tricky business unless it is under absolutely controlled circumstances. The windowsill does not qualify as such a place. It can be several weeks from the time a pot is brought indoors, to a month before the flowers show, depending on the conditions. And it varies from genus to genus, as well. Crocus and the diminutive snow iris burst into bloom in a very short time. Little *Iris reticulata* always surprises me. There isn't much room to hide behind the thin daggers of leaves, but suddenly, out of nowhere, appear the buds. In a day or two they have unfurled.

The time to move a pot from the window to the place where it can best be seen is when the buds show color. Nothing can stop the show now. It is unwise, of course, to tempt fate too much, by placing the pot on say, the radiator. Equally bad choices include the mantle or near the blast of the furnace. The top of the television set is even more inappropriate, and placing

POTS OF CROCUS AND SNOW IRIS, RECENTLY BROUGHT INDOORS FROM THEIR DARK "WINTER" IN THE GARAGE, THRIVE IN BRIGHT, COOL CONDITIONS.

any plant there is, in fact, a horticultural faux pas of the worst order. Appliances and plants do not mix.

Some flowers last longer than others, and many gardeners shuttle their bulbs with a short bloom season to a cool window or porch every night, as this will help to extend a bloom's duration.

A friend of mine got caught by the change of seasons. She had visited the garden center, and with visions of her spring garden fueling her buying frenzy she loaded the trunk of her car with bulbs. Important matters called her out of town, and a blizzard greeted her return. Fall was gone, and so was the opportunity to plant the garden. The bulbs sat in the trunk in the cool garage. She rediscovered them shortly before Christmas. She called me in panic.

I lugged over spare pots and soil, and we spent a harried afternoon potting more bulbs than most people grow in a decade. We stored them in the crawl space beneath her house and crossed our fingers. The flowers came in waves, as she lined them in her sun room, and then every window in the house. She was the most popular lady in town that spring, delivering pots to everyone she knew.

AFTERLIFE

I've always thought it unfortunate that so many books recommend discarding the bulbs after they've flowered indoors once. The bulbs are so weakened, they say—so thoroughly expended from the tortures of forcing—that they are no longer of value. This goes against the natural, nurturing grain of most gardeners. I don't know about the atrocities they went through in the houses of those authorities (perhaps they sat the bulbs on the television set), but in my house they are fed and watered, and the foliage is allowed to grow in a sunny spot until it has ripened, turning first yellow then brown, so that it can restore as much energy to the bulbs as possible.

With containers, any worry about foliage becomes moot. After garden flowers fade, gardeners fret over the subsequent death of the leaves. Just as the garden enters what is to many the most important and flamboyant period—of peonies, poppies, and delphiniums—the withering yellow leaves of tulips, daffodils, and fritillaries in particular, mar the picture. Some gardeners become obsessed with these leaves, considering them a personal tweak in the nose. They braid daffodil leaves, for instance—a silly practice of questionable horticultural merit—or worse, cut them off prematurely before they have ripened. This does insure, however, sparse flowering in successive years and the eventual death

of the bulbs, permanently resolving the problem.

Container-grown bulbs solve this dilemma. After flowering, the bulbs can be moved to a less conspicuous location where the leaves finish their life cycle out of sight. The bulbs may be given to friends who worry less about the yellowing demise of the leaves to plant in their gardens.

Sure, they were a bit crowded in those pots, but the soil was rich, and their lives were, as far as I can determine, not much different from those of their cousins in the garden, except those in the house did not get their stems broken or find their faces in the mud after a heavy rain or late snow storm.

Most bulbs that have been grown indoors can continue to lead perfectly normal lives if they have been well treated. I would not replant them directly outside the front door or in any prominent spot, for they do seem to need a year or two to get the wind back in their sails. This lack of vigor in the garden can be a blessing, though. Hyacinths, for instance, that bloomed indoors, look all the better when they are placed next to other plants, for the stalks are less crowded and the effect is more graceful.

DIMINUTIVE SNOW IRIS TAKE CENTER STAGE, INCLUDING DEEP BLUE
IRIS HISTRIOIDES 'GEORGE', YELLOW I. DANFORDIAE, AND PALE BLUE I. RETICULATA
'NATASHA' WITH 'HAWERA' NARCISSUS.

Most of the bulbs may be replanted during the spring—after the flowers are gone and while other folks are busy braiding the leaves—while they are still actively growing, if the gardener is careful. The advantage to transplanting them in the spring is that, at this point, it is much easier to picture how they will look with existing plants.

The spring garden is full of chores, and it is often easier to postpone transplanting the bulbs until late summer or fall. In this case, simply leave the bulbs in their pots. Let them bask in the spring shade of just-leafing trees. Sunshine, water, and applications of well-balanced fertilizer plump the bulbs. As the leaves wither, completing the year's cycle, gradually withhold water by increasing the intervals between waterings until the pots go bone-dry. Then the pots can be hidden from view if the unsightly leaves offend.

Many bulbs and corms, such as tulips and crocus, revel in a good summer baking, but there's no need to really cook them in the hot sun. They can be left in their pots and stored in the garage or under a bench if other garden tasks take priority. Or dig them out, cut off old withered growth, and air-dry them in a dry,

ventilated basement or on the porch. After a few days of curing, place them in mesh, paper bags, or even old stockings, and store them in a cool, dry, dark spot.

I've never saved bulbs simply for the sake of frugality. It seems wasteful to discard something useful, something that can add to the garden. Free bulbs, I consider them, and gardeners can rarely turn down a bargain, though in most cases they should. In this case, I know where the bulbs came from and what treatment they've had.

An out-of-the-way corner of my garden has benefitted greatly from my leftover bulbs. I call this area the wilderness, for it is left to its own devices, getting little care. The ferns, tree peonies, hypericums, and hostas under a maple are interplanted with a hodgepodge of flowers that have graced the house over the years, and it's a pretty hodgepodge. Happenstance was the designer, not me. Tulips, daffodils, grape hyacinths, crocus, and squills pop up throughout the spring, and I feel no guilt—as I might in raiding the show borders—in snitching a few for bouquets. That's a hefty return of pleasure for the bulbs I've been advised to discard.

BLOOMING AHEAD OF THEIR COUNTERPARTS IN THE GARDEN, POT-GROWN CROCUS, SNOW IRIS, AND 'APRICOT BEAUTY' TULIPS BASK WITH TENDER BEGONIAS ⟩ SCILLA PERUVIANA, **AND PERSIAN BUTTERCUPS.**

ALLIUM

LILY LEEK

TOO AGGRESSIVE IN SOME GARDENS, CONTAINED ALLIUM MOLY **IS SAFELY ENJOYED FOR ITS FOOT-TALL CLUSTERS OF FLOWERS ABOVE BLUE-GREEN FOLIAGE.**

Golden garlic, *A. moly*, has been a favorite in English gardens since the seventeenth century, when it was introduced from southern France and eastern Spain. Sometimes called the lily leek, it has a reputation for multiplying all too well, so it may be safely enjoyed on the window ledge or patio.

Pink-flowered *A. oreophilum* (formerly known as *A. ostrowskianum*) is another attractive choice for the windowsill. This native of the Caucasus and Siberia has been cultivated since the early Victorian period, and is beloved for its carmine tint and diminutive six-inch height.

Few plants are as dramatic in a pot as the Turkestan onion, *A. karataviense*. The leaves are noted for their unusual width and blue-gray coloration streaked with burgundy red, especially on the edges. Above them—on short, stout stalks —rise the spherical heads of creamy-white flowers that can be as large as five inches in diameter.

At least a dozen more species should be tried as container plants, including the lavender star-of-Persia, *A. christophii* (formerly *A. albopilosum*) and lilac-purple *A. aflatunense*. I do have difficulty picturing *A. giganteum*, that freakish, four-foot purple lollipop of nature, in a pot. Although it can be done, it might look just a wee bit out of scale at all but a coronation.

ANEMONE

WINDFLOWER

Vibrant petals fluttering, anemones take their name from the Greek word for the wind, *anemonos*. The hills of this ancient land are home to Grecian windflower, *Anemone blanda*. It has secured a place in rock gardens world-wide and this spring bloomer makes a good container subject as well. The single, daisy-like flowers bloom in shades of pink, white, and Wedgwood blue. The variety 'White Splendor' is understandably popular for its larger, pristine blossoms. The flowers measure almost two inches across, and bloom on four-inch stems over divided deep green leaves.

Florist's anemone, *A. coronaria* from southern Europe, has three-inch-wide flowers of scarlet, purple, or white atop eighteen-inch stems. The 'de Caen' strain, named for the French district where it was raised, features large single blooms; the 'St. Brigid' strain is double.

Pot tubers in fall and leave outdoors in shade. After a frost, move pots indoors and fertilize and water liberally. Finding the right spot can be tough; it has to be bright, cool, and humid—an English castle with skylights would be ideal.

FLORIST'S ANEMONES DON'T NEED THE SAME COLD TREATMENT AS A. BLANDA.

BRODIAEA

BLUE DICKS

Named for the Scottish horticulturalist James Brodie (1744-1824), most species of *Brodiaea* are rare in commerce. The most common, *B. laxa* (also known as *Triteleia laxa*), valued for its deep violet blue flowers, has been grown since its discovery in 1832. It sometimes goes by the folk name blue dicks, for which I can offer no explanation and am reluctant to speculate. It has also been known as Ithuriel's spear, named for the angel in Milton's *Paradise Lost*.

B. laxa produces umbels of funnel-shaped, six-petaled flowers, up to an inch across, on wiry stems up to two feet tall. The plant grows just two opposing, linear leaves that reach from twelve to eighteen inches in length. The selected form 'Queen Fabiola' grows on longer, stronger stems. The vigorous hybrid *B. × tubergenii* carries large umbels of pale blue flowers with deeper-toned exteriors. *B. lactea* (*Triteleia hyacinthina*) is distinguished by milk-white flowers on eighteen-inch stems. Closely spaced corms perform well in pots, with moisture in winter and spring, and a dry period in late summer and fall.

CAMASSIA

QUAMASH

From the scant attention they receive in today's garden, one would never suspect the crucial role the bulbs of *Camassia* played in the old West. Native to North America with the exception of one South American species, *Camassia*—called quamash by Native Americans—was a staple food of many western tribes. Quamash fields were fiercely defended as tribal property, for the bulbs meant survival.

White explorers, settlers, and their flocks took advantage of the bulbs as well; the Lewis and Clark expedition (1803-1806), for instance, depended on quamash as their sole source of food at times. In a last, desperate war in 1877, Chief Joseph and his Nez Perce warriors attempted, in vain, to drive the encroaching white man from their quamash grounds.

It is possible to grow a pot of western history, appreciating the pretty lavender blue flowers that spring from the fabled bulbs. The bulbs, it should be noted, are poisonous until they are cooked, so gardeners should probably confine themselves to enjoying the sight of the flowers.

C. quamash, formerly known as *C. esculenta*, is oddly named. Since the genus name is derived from the common name, the name is essentially repeated twice, like saying *Petunia petunia*.

Native to moist meadows of Utah, Montana, and the Pacific Northwest, *C. quamash* ranks among the prettiest of wild flowers, but it readily adapts to garden and container culture. Flower stalks from one to two feet in height emerge from the linear, green or gray-green basal foliage. Starry flowers, up to forty in a raceme, bloom in succession from the bottom up. The effect is like that of a giant squill, to which *Camassia* is closely related. Varieties from deep violet-blue to almost white have been selected. Because of their stature, the flower stalks sometimes need support to keep them upright.

AN INCONSPICUOUS "GIRDLE" SUPPORTS STEMS OF CAMASSIA **DISPLAYED AT THE PHILADELPHIA FLOWER SHOW,** *left.* **WISPY** BRODIAEA IAXA **IS PAIRED WITH PLUMP TUBEROUS BEGONIAS,** *above left.*

CHIONODOXA

GLORY-OF-THE-SNOW

The botanical name for this spring charmer is remarkably apt and succinct. From the Greek *chion*, glory, and *doxa*, snow, it conjures images of the petite flowers blooming on the mountainsides of Turkey and Crete. *Chionodoxa* is a word that does not trip easily off the tongue, so gardeners opt for glory-of-the-snow.

The starry flowers of *C. luciliae*, the only species commonly grown, are borne in racemes on stems four to eight inches above the ground. Up to ten flowers—true-blue, shading to white in the interior—cluster on each stem.

Large bulbs often produce multiple flower stems over the sparse leaves of dark green. The selected form 'Pink Giant' grows taller than the type with correspondingly larger, baby-doll pink flowers, a little more than an inch across. A pure white form can sometimes be found in commerce. Glory-of-the-snow blooms for up to three weeks, and is especially pretty paired with 'February Gold' daffodils, which blooms simultaneously if planted at the same time and grown together.

GLORY-OF-THE-SNOW IS ALL THE MORE PRETTY AT CLOSE RANGE, *left*. AS IF LIFTED FROM A WOODLAND FLOOR, A CLUMP OF LILY-OF-THE-VALLEY IS CARPETED BY BABY TEARS, *above right*. A POT OF CONVALLARIA GROUPED WITH POLKA-DOT PLANT, IVY, AND SPIDER PLANT, *right*, CAN BE TRANSPLANTED OUTDOORS AFTER FLOWERING.

CONVALLARIA

LILY-OF-THE-VALLEY

Legions of fans treasure the sweet, pure scent of the flowers of lily-of-the-valley. Native to most of temperate Europe, *Convallaria majalis* is aptly named, for in Latin, *convallis* means valley, the favored habitat of the plants, while *majalis* denotes that it flowers in May. Professional growers have become adept at holding the tuberous roots, called pips or crowns, in cold storage to grow the plants for bridal bouquets at any season; the home gardener must stick with the winter and early spring. Drinking in the exquisite fragrance is the reward for a couple of months of winter chill.

Sir Walter Scott wrote of "Sweet May Lilies" and legend holds that the flowers sprang from the tears of Mary Magdalen shed over the death of Christ. The tears flowed down the valley where they came to life. A member of the lily family, *Convallaria* has clustered white flowers that dangle from stems six to eight inches tall. A selected form displays pale pink blossoms. An unusual variety, 'Aureo-variegata' sports attractive leaves with longitudinal stripes of cream yellow. A rare double-flowered form should remain that way.

It takes four weeks for the flowers to bloom once they are brought into the warmth of the house. Many catalogues offer pre-cooled pips that cut the whole operation down to four weeks.

Native in the wild from the Mediterranean to Afghanistan, at least eighty species of *Crocus* tempt gardeners. Beloved since ancient times, most species bloom in late winter or spring, although its name would suggest otherwise. The name comes from the ancient Greek word *krokos* or saffron, a substance derived from autumn-flowering *C. sativus*. Crocuses grow from corms, and indoors the flowers last longest if grown in very cool conditions. Their chilling requirements are modest compared to most spring bloomers; corner cutters may succeed with as little as six weeks of cold treatment, although ten is ideal.

Plump Dutch crocus were developed by industrious Hollanders from *C. vernus*, native to central and southern Europe. From royal purple to golden yellow and pure white, selected varieties exhibit flowers up to six inches high in a wide range of tints. Yellow varieties, for some undetermined reason, flower less well in containers than those of other coloration. Favorite cultivated varieties include white 'Jeanne d'Arc', dark purple 'Flower Record', and lilac-striped 'Pickwick'. Pots of Dutch crocus on the winter windowsill keep many gardeners' spirits from flagging.

To stop with these, however, is to deny oneself the charms of an enormous genus with charm to spare. Dainty snow crocus, only three to four inches tall, deserve equal space in the window. Derived principally from *C. chrysanthus*, snow crocus offer an intriguing array of colors and patterns. Some blossoms are marked with pencil-thin stripes, featherings, and blotches, while others display clear tones of white, cream, yellow, blue, and purple. Aptly-named selections include 'Blue Peter', 'Cream Beauty', 'Snow Bunting', 'Goldilocks', maroon and cream 'Ladykiller', and deep blue 'Zenith'.

The five-inch flowers of *C. etruscus*, found in the wild only in the Etruscan Mountains of Italy, are a lustrous silver-gray striped with deeper lilac, with a yellow throat. Those of fragrant *C. sieberi*, from Greece and Crete, are shaded lilac blue with

a deep tangerine throat, while in the selected variety 'Firefly' the outside petals are nearly white. *C. tommasinianus*, native to the Balkan Peninsula, is distinguished by a beard of fine hairs in the interior of each flower. The slender, delicate flowers, six inches high, can be spoiled by wind or rain in the garden, so the pale lavender-blue petals are all the more appreciated indoors.

Scotch crocus, *C. biflorus*, typically produces fragrant, four-inch blossoms with white or pale lavender petals with striking purplish-brown feathering. Selections from this species, native to Italy—not Scotland—are white or buff yellow with various degrees of purple on the outsides of the petals. Cloth-of-gold, *C. angustifolius* (also called *C. susiana*) is better suited to its name. The deep yellow flowers from Russia, only two inches tall, are tinted mahogany red on the outside.

CROCUS

PLUMP 'PICKWICK' CROCUS CHASE AWAY WINTER BLUES, OPENING WIDE WHEN PLACED NEAR A WINDOW OR BRIGHT LAMP.

FRITILLARIA

FRITILLARY

The diverse *Fritillaria* contains giants and midgets. The genus, native mainly to mountainous regions of the northern hemisphere, is notable for its unusual flower forms and bizarre, if not brilliant, coloration. The markings on some flowers led to the name *Fritillaria*, derived from the Latin *fritillus*, a checkerboard. Nowhere are those unique markings more apparent than in *F. meleagris*, indigenous from England to southwest Asia. Aside from the giant species known as the crown imperial, *F. imperialis*, which possesses a peculiar foxy odor making it unsuitable for indoor culture, *F. meleagris* is the best-known species.

Colored maroon-red or grayish-purple, the squared, pendant flowers are checkered in a lighter shade. This pattern has always reminded me of the sportscoats of early rock 'n' rollers of the '50s. Long in cultivation, *F. meleagris* came to be called the guinea hen flower or snake's head. Growing from six to ten inches in height, the pendant blossoms dangle on thin stems with scant, thin, gray-green leaves.

Persian bells, *F. persica*, commands attention for its stately stalks growing to two feet or more. Its twisting leaves are the color of a *verdis gris* patina on weathered copper. The upper third of the stem carries blossoms of a unique color: plum-purple with a waxy "bloom" like that of grapes. The understated yet riveting combination of leaf and flower coloration is enhanced by companion plants of peach or pink tones, such as 'Gipsy Queen' hyacinths or double 'Angelique' tulips. Native to the Cypress, Turkey, and Iraq, *F. persica* is often represented by the robust, taller form 'Adiyaman', named for the town near which it was discovered.

Also native to Turkey, eight-inch-tall *F. michailovskyi* bears blossoms of maroon-red, the ends of the petals appearing to have been dipped in a pot of brilliant yellow paint. It resembles a tulip with a nodding head, and has become a favorite of fritillary fanciers. Indigenous to the same region, *F. uva-vulpis* (often confused with similar *F. assyriaca*) bears pendulous violet-maroon bells with striking interiors of golden bronze. The vigorous species grows to a foot in height and its leaves are blue green.

Fritillaries pose no special growing challenges, but the bulbs are subject to dessication since they are not cloaked in protective tunics. Plant immediately in gritty, humusy soil.

THE DUSKY PLUM FLOWERS OF PERSIAN
BELLS, *left*, CONTRAST WITH 'ANGELIQUE' TULIPS.
NODDING GUINEA HEN FLOWERS, *above*,
ARE CHARMINGLY CHECKERED.

GALANTHUS

SNOWDROP

AFTER SNOWDROPS FADE THEY CAN BE TRANSPLANTED TO A SHADY SPOT WHERE THEY OFTEN NATURALIZE WITH ABANDON.

One of the first bulbs to signal the transition of the seasons, the tiny snowdrop has long been cherished for its delicate beauty. *Galanthus nivalis*, a wild flower throughout Europe, has inspired poets and gardeners alike for centuries, sometimes to excess. The scientific name is derived from the Greek words *gala*, milk, and *anthos*, flower—obviously for the color of the blossoms—while *nivalis* means of the snow. Its placement in the showy amaryllis family is surprising.

In England, the nodding six-petaled, green-tipped blossoms are called the fair-maids-of-February, and nowhere else do they create such a flurry of excitement. There must be a score of selected varieties although the discrepancies are miniscule, except for the double form. Even the species, including *G. elwesii* and *G. byzantinus*, both from Turkey, differ little from each other. Some authorities regard all varieties, hybrids, and species as one species, *G. nivalis*, and credit the enormous geographical distribution and length of cultivation in gardens for differences.

All forms of snowdrop grow easily in pots with little coaxing, but they should be planted touching each other—bulb to bulb—or the show will be scant. Less than six inches high, the flowers echo the white of the frosted panes.

The passion for hyacinths goes back to the days of the ancients. The name comes from the Greeks, and commemorates fallen Hyakinthos, from whose blood, legend has it, the flowers sprang. The handsome young man had been practicing discus-throwing with his god friend Apollo, when one of Apollo's shots was blown by a gust of wind (rumored to have been the work of Zephyrus, god of the west wind) striking Hyakinthos in the temple (of his head). An alarming number of Apollo's friends and lovers ended up as plants.

Selected by centuries of breeding from the wild species *Hyacinthus orientalis*, native to the eastern Mediterranean region, modern varieties scarcely resemble their ancestors. It's quite remarkable how the original wild hyacinth was transformed into a buxom beauty. Only about fifteen loosely spaced white or pale mauve flowers occur on the foot-tall stems of the original plant. The wildlings still waft their potent perfume on the hillsides of their native lands in spring, while their made-over cousins grace civic center displays and accompany polite dinner conversation.

As different from the original species as today's automobiles are from Henry Ford's Model T, modern hyacinths are the product of Dutch breeding mainly since the seventeenth century.

HYACINTHUS

HYACINTH

FRENCH ROMAN HYACINTHS POSSESS A
WILD CHARM AND GENTLE FRAGRANCE

The Victorians, in turn, were mad for hyacinths. A simple procedure—to place a bulb in a glass of water and watch it grow—it became all the rage. Kept in a dark, cool cupboard until the glass was filled with roots and the flower bud had become visible, the hyacinths were brought into subdued light and warmer temperatures for a week. The flowers then took an honored place in the parlor window. Special vases, which came to be known as hyacinth glasses, became part of the contents of every Victorian china cabinet. The distinctive hourglass shape was designed to keep just the bottom of the bulb in contact with the water chamber below it. Perhaps it was just coincidence that the shape of the hyacinth glass echoed the ideal female figure of the day.

The magic of the water-grown hyacinth continues to delight. As with all seemingly simple procedures, however, things can go awry. Special pre-cooled bulbs, available from garden centers, give the best results in water. A small lump of charcoal (available at any pet store that stocks tropical fish) keeps the water from turning into a slimy mire.

The cool, dark place for chilling must not be too cool, as I learned one harsh winter when I'd stashed the hyacinth bulbs in their glasses in a closet on the north side of the house. Checking on their progress one chilly morning, I found the water had frozen, bursting the vases, leaving a soggy mess of broken glass and stranded bulbs. I scooped up the rooted bulbs and ransacked the kitchen for suitable jars. I finally settled on a hodgepodge of containers with the openings appropriate to the task, including old-fashioned canning jars. Their bubbled, aqua-tinted glass complemented the pink blossoms (which had suffered no damage), and I've preferred them ever since.

Hyacinths can be grown in soil, of course, with the prerequisite cold treatment. Once again, growers deliver treated bulbs that have been through a "curing" process. Dug early from the growing fields, the bulbs receive several weeks of warm temperatures to encourage development of the embryonic flowers, and are then held in carefully controlled cold storage. These bulbs, planted as soon as they become available in September, require only ten to twelve weeks of cold treatment, and can be in bloom at Christmas. The gardener who isn't in as much of a rush may plant untreated hyacinth bulbs at any time in the fall, although the length of winter chill required is several weeks longer.

The Victorian period was the zenith for the hyacinth. Hundreds of cultivated varieties kept the parlor air sweet. A range of kaleidoscopic colors—white, yellow, pink, lavender, purple, and red—ensured their popularity, as did double-flowered forms. Some of these heirlooms survive to this day.

The original wild hyacinth is on the comeback trail, and is sometimes preferred by antique-flower enthusiasts who prefer its delicate, unimproved aspect to that of formal Dutch

APRICOT 'GIPSY QUEEN' DWARFS HEIRLOOM 'DISTINCTION', *above right.* **'LADY DERBY' BLOSSOMS IN CANNING JARS**, *below right.*

varieties. A pretty white form of the wild species found in southern France, *H. orientalis* var. *albulus*, is often called the French Roman hyacinth. It possesses a gentle fragrance with a hint of cinnamon. Multiflora hyacinths capitalize on the desire for simpler forms. Surgically altered by cutting away the basal plate, multifloras produce smaller multiple stems. All adapt readily to pot culture, offering the gardener an alternative to the stately standards. Should anyone endure a winter without the scent of hyacinths?

IPHEION

SPRING STAR FLOWER

Native to temperate eastern South America, *Ipheion uniflora* (formerly *Triteleia uniflora*, and closely related to the whole *Brodiaea* clan) is the only member of its genus in general cultivation. One of the so-called "minor" bulbs, as horticultural categorization has long held, its pale lavender-blue flowers possess a symmetrical beauty, earning the folk name spring star flower. The one-inch diameter flowers, one per stem, carry a slight, sweet scent, but the grassy leaves, when bruised, smell of onions.

A selected form, 'Wisely Blue', was discovered in the gardens of the Royal Horticultural Society in England. It bears deep blue flowers nearly two inches across.

Water bulbs sparingly after potting them in sandy loam. Sprouted plants revel in a bright, cool window and fertilization should be slight if at all. After flowering, dry them off gradually; they may remain in the same pot for several years with an annual top-dressing. The bulbs are easily transplanted to the garden after flowering, either while still in active growth or while dormant.

IRIS

THE SUBTLE HUE OF SPRING STAR FLOWER, *left*, MATCHES CONFEDERATE VIOLETS AND BIRD'S EYE VERONICA. FORMS OF IRIS RETICULATA, *above*, SHOW MOODY BLUES.

The Greek goddess of the rainbow was winged, silk-clad Iris. I think that pretty much explains the choice of name for a genus comprised of about three hundred species, which populate the temperate regions of the northern hemisphere. I dare say I haven't yet encountered one of these winged, silky creations that wasn't lovely. For practical purposes, *Iris* is divided into two main groups: bulbous and rhizomatous. Species of both make outstanding container plants.

Iris reticulata grows wild in the Caucasus and Iran. This snow iris makes an excellent container plant, and is all the more appreciated since its diminutive size rarely invites face-to-face examination in the garden. The thin leaves form a corral around the graceful flowers. The flowers themselves are composed of erect standards and falls painted with a raised orange or yellow ridge bordered white.

Selection has produced a range of colors—all of them pretty—from violet, reddish-purple, sky blue, and royal blue to pale blue and milky white. A similar species, Turkish *I. histrioides* blooms bigger and bluer. The flowers of *I. reticulata* measure about two inches in diameter, on plants six to eight inches tall.

I. danfordiae is its yellow counterpart. This Turkish relative has been cultivated since before the turn of the century. The fragrant yellow flowers are spotted with random green markings. They rise just four inches out of the pot.

Iris bucharica grows on stony hillsides in Central Asia. The lightly fragrant, yellow-and-white flowers are set off by shiny, bright green foliage on twelve-inch plants. The arrangement of the leaves, set at overlapping angles one above another, adds to its beauty. The double- or triple-nosed bulbs produce multiple stems, with each stem bearing up to seven flowers, each, in turn, up to two inches across. The standards are usually white, while the yellow falls bear a deeper blotch.

Many other iris preform well in pots, especially Dutch iris, so familiar as cut flowers, as well as Juno or Oncocyclus species and types, especially for the cool greenhouse.

The distinction between bulbous and rhizotomous species and varieties is not especially important in growing irises in containers. Many iris take to pot culture, so the logical choices for the home gardeners are those of diminutive size, or those that may be innappropriate for the gardener's particular soil or climate. The Oncocyclus types, for example, prosper in a

IRIS BUCHARICA **BLOOMS WITH** SCILLA SIBERICA **AND** TULIPA LINIFOLIA.

simulation of their Middle Eastern dry summer baking and clay soil—no mean feat in Seattle or Secaucus—but easier to accomplish in pots than in the garden.

Dwarf bearded iris make rewarding subjects for pots because of their beauty, fragrance, and ease of culture. Gardeners who object to iris foliage after the plants have bloomed will find that growing them in pots makes it possible to let the leaves grow out of sight. They may be planted in pots as in the garden—in late summer—and stored in the cold frame.

LEUCOJUM
SNOWFLAKE

DWARF BEARDED IRIS CONSORT WITH JOHNNY-JUMP-UPS AND NARCISSUS, *left.* **SUMMER SNOWFLAKE,** *above,* **IS A SUBTLE BEAUTY.**

Snowflakes are related to snowdrops, and if that weren't reason enough for confusion between *Leucojum* and *Galanthus*, the flowers of both are pendulous, white, and green-tipped (and nobody can figure out what the little charmers are doing in the amaryllis family).

Careful observation reveals that the flower petals of snowflakes are level (those of snowdrops are of unequal length), and *Leucojum* starts with an "l." Aside from that, snowflakes possess their own distinctive beauty, resembling tiny inflated parachutes.

Spring snowflake, *L. vernum*, grows wild in southern Europe. Hippocrates, he of the fabled oath, knew the flower and called it *leucoeion*, meaning white eye. Its usually solitary pristine blossoms appear on six-inch stems in the late winter (as do those of snowdrops). No wonder confusion is rampant. Summer snowflake, *L. aestivum*, native to central Europe, is distinguished by its tall stature, up to twenty inches tall, and later blooming period. Its straight stems arch near the top, displaying the blossoms like chiming bells. Both species grow from bulbs clad in brown tunics, perform reliably in pots, and thrive in organically rich, moisture-retentive soil.

LILIUM

LILY

ASIATIC HYBRID LILY 'FAUN' ECHOS
TUBEROUS BEGONIAS AND COLEUS.

The first acquaintance most gardeners make with the lily family is at Easter. The white trumpets of *L. longiflorum* blast a sweet perfume that has become firmly entrenched since the turn of the century as part of the holiday. Native to the islands south of Japan, millions of so-called Easter lilies command the spring-flower market.

It is not the only lily for indoor spring pleasure. Brilliant Asiatic hybrids, derived mainly from species native to China, offer a wide range of colors. Thousands of floriferous hybrids have been produced by American and Dutch enthusiasts in the past forty years. Those that work best for indoor pot culture grow two feet tall or less. Most are not fragrant, but they make up for it with lovely flowers shaded in every color except blue.

It is the rare gardener who attempts to grow Easter lilies at home, especially considering their wide, inexpensive availability shortly before the holiday. Cool, bright conditions prolong the life and display of store-bought plants. *L. longiflorum* is on the tender side, so only gardeners with relatively mild winter temperatures succeed when they plant their purchases outdoors afterwards.

Hardy Asiatic hybrids require ten to twelve

weeks of chilling after the bulbs are potted in fibrous, well-drained soil during late autumn. Very sunny but cool conditions help to develop stocky, robust plants. Aphids sometimes infest the plants but are easily controlled with a dousing of soap suds. After the bulbs' spring fling, the foliage is grown on as long as possible and fertilized. They may be transplanted in spring or fall to the garden for years of beauty in most parts of the country.

EASTER LILIES ARE DISPLAYED WITH- OUT GLITSY FOIL WRAP AND BOWS, TO NO ONE'S REGRET.

MUSCARI

GRAPE HYACINTH

A PERFECT POT OF 'BLUE SPIKE' GRAPE HYACINTHS GRABS THE SPOTLIGHT
AT THE PHILADELPHIA FLOWER SHOW.

The grape hyacinth mingles with lily-of-the-valley in the childhood memories of many. The clustered bubbles of bloom, possess an irresistible scent, and are aptly named from the Latin *muscus*, musk.

The most common species, *M. armeniacum*, became an instant favorite upon its introduction to western cultivation from the Balkan Mountains in 1878. Up to eight inches in height, the flowering stems, rising from thin, grasslike leaves, bear blue flowers with a purple cast and a white rim at the mouth. The variety 'Blue Spike' offers showy double flowers.

Native to France and Italy, *M. botryoides*, similar to *M. armeniacum* in most respects, is most often represented in pots and gardens by its pretty white form 'Album'. *M. comosum* is likewise represented by a selected variety, in this case 'Plumosum'. Its frilly mauve flowers earn it the name feathered hyacinth.

Charming in its simplicity, grape hyacinth makes the best of mixers—like good party guests—combining well with tulips and daffodils in staged baskets and jardiniere.

MINIATURE DAFFODIL 'LITTLE BEAUTY' IS TOPPED BY 'HAPPY FAMILY' TULIPS, *above*. 'BRIDAL CROWN' TOWERS ABOVE 'QUAIL', *right*.

NARCISSUS
DAFFODIL

Narcissus is the quintessential flower of spring. Widespread in Europe, western Asia, and North Africa, the genus displays an array of diverse flowers; although the image of yellow trumpet daffodils like classic 'King Alfred' often spring to mind. Has any other flower been more often described as "cheerful"?

Strange then, that the name comes from the often told morose myth of the boy Narcissus. A handsome fellow, he was pursued by many a young maiden but spurned them all, including the nymph Echo, who pined away in seclusion until all that was left of her was a plaintive voice. The gods heard the prayers of the miserable maidens calling for a punishment for Narcissus. The goddess Nemesis, in charge of such things, arranged for him to catch sight of his reflection as he stooped to drink from a stream. He was so enamoured with what he saw, never leaving the spot, that he eventually sprouted roots and became a flower. Moralists throughout the ages have looked to the narcissistic tale for inspiration.

The popular name daffodil appears to be a derivation from the Old English *affodylle*, in turn stemming from the Greek *asphodelus*, a name now given to an entirely different plant, the asphodel. Some gardeners use the name jonquil in place of daffodil or *Narcissus*, although it usually refers to the wild species *N. jonquilla* of Spain and Portugal. With up to seventy species and thousands of hybrids and cultivated varietes, a bit of name overlap is understandable and harmless.

To bring order out of chaos, *Narcissus* are classified into twelve divisions based mainly on their flower forms, especially length of the cup, and their kinship. Most gardeners, however, think of four groups: large-flowered daffodils, miniatures, clustered varieties, and paperwhites (tender bulbs covered in Chapter Four.) Of the remaining three, they offer flowers in various sizes, heights, and shapes and almost all of them take to container growing.

The standard large-flowered yellow prototype is an old favorite, while varieties with single or bicolored cups and petals expand the range to include white, cream, chartreuse, orange, and pale apricot or pink tones.

Small-flowering and miniature varieties are enchanting. Favorites include 'February Gold', 'Jack Snipe', 'Jenny', 'Jumblie', 'Minnow', and 'Tête-à-tête'. Clustered and mutiflowering types 'Bridal Crown', 'Cheerfulness', 'Geranium', 'Hawera', and 'St. Agnes' carry sprays of tiny blossoms, often with a delicious, understated fragrance.

SMALL DAFFODILS, SUCH AS N. CANALICULATUS, BEAR CLUSTERS OF WINSOME BLOSSOMS.

RHODOHYPOXIS

ROSE STAR

The Drakensberg Mountains of South Africa are home to rose star, *Rhodohypoxis*. Just a few inches tall, the six-petaled flowers possess an innocent charm, as if drawn by a child. Their color is white, pale pink, or rose, and the stamens are hidden in the centers, adding further to their simplicity. Each plant produces many flowers. The leaves and stems bristle with fine hairs.

Rhodohypoxis combines *rhodon*, rose, with the genus name *Hypoxis*. These related plants from Africa, Australia, and North America are often called star grass or fairy stars. *R. baurii* is the only species commercially available and may, indeed, be the only one that is not extinct. The cormlike roots are planted closely together in fall and chilled for ten or twelve weeks, and care must be taken that temperatures never fall below freezing. Peaty, sandy soil is a must. The plants go dormant after flowering and may be left undisturbed in their pots for several years.

ROSE STARS, *above*, **MAY BE GROWN IN THE SAME POT FOR SEVERAL YEARS.**

SCILLA

SQUILL

The true blue color of Siberian squill, *Scilla siberica*, enthralls lovers of blue flowers. Its six-petaled nodding blossoms, usually arranged five or six to a stem, are particular favorites of mine. Their haze of rich blue set against a frosted pane is one of the prettiest sights of winter.

Siberian squill is just the tip of the iceberg of the genus *Scilla*, native to the Old World. Named by Hippocrates, *scilla* means "to harm," for the bulbs of some species contain potent poisons. *S. siberica* is actually native to Asia Minor and the Caucasus, and has been perennially popular since its introduction in 1796. A relative newcomer to western horticulture, free-flowering *S. tubergeniana* from Iran sports white flowers with just the palest of blue casts, with a relatively darker blue stripe running down the center of each petal.

It blooms so early in many gardens that it is often lost in the snow, giving indoor pot culture a decided advantage. Gardeners will not to be happy to hear that the plant has been renamed *S. miczenkoana*, and may choose to feign ignorant bliss.

Spanish and English bluebells, *S. campanulata* and *S. non-scripta* have been tossed from genus to genus like horticultural footballs. Here they are stubbornly included in *Scilla*, although they were,

MEADOW SQUILL, *above*, **IS A WILD FLOWER OF EASTERN EUROPE.**

for a time, transferred to *Agraphis*, then *Endymion*, and now, to gardeners' dismay, to *Hyacinthoides*. Long beloved and extensively cultivated, these similar bulbs—whatever their names—bloom on lissome, arching stems from a foot to twenty inches tall in shades of blue, pink, or white. Often naturalized in orchards and wooded areas, bluebells benefit from rich, organic soil when grown in pots.

Meadow squill, *S. pratensis*, is indigenous to the Slavic republics and has been cultivated since the beginning of the Victorian Age. The tiny lilac-blue flowers, softly scented, are bunched on stems elongating as the blossoms open to as tall as a foot. Not reliably hardy in cold winter areas, meadow squill delights windowsill gardeners who might otherwise not have the pleasure of its company outdoors in April and May. The bulbs may be chilled at higher temperatures than most—45° or 50° F. is ideal—making a basement cupboard a suitable place for its rooting period.

Cuban lily, *S. peruviana*, bears two misleading names. Aside from not being a lily, it is not native to Cuba or Peru, but to Spain and Portugal. Spaniards probably introduced the bulbs to the New World, where they flourished and naturalized. The six-inch flower heads, packed with as many as a hundred flowers, are the most impressive of the squills. The bulbs are expensive and worth it. Violet blue or white flowers open over a long period on foot-tall stems, enhanced by a rosette of spear-shaped leaves. It, too, is not hardy in cold climes, and must be protected from freezing and treated like meadow squill.

Puschkinia scilloides, native to Turkey, is called striped squill due to its similarities to its cousins, especially *S. siberica*. The Russian Count Appollos Apollosvich Mussin-Puschkin first collected the bulbs that bear his name (at least part of it) early in the nineteenth century. What makes striped squill worth growing is its color. The blossoms are very pale, almost white, but the deeper-toned stripes are turquoise blue. The overall impression is of soft aqua foam. The bulbs, planted and chilled in a standard bulb pan, can be left in the same pot and rebloomed for several years.

AN UNDERSTATED INDOOR "WHITE GARDEN" FEATURES SCILLA SIBERICA '**ALBA', PANSIES, PLUM BLOSSOMS,** BLETILLA STRIATA, **AND SHOOTING STAR,** DODECATHEON MEADIA.

TULIPA
~
TULIP

Give a child a box of crayons and ask him or her to draw a flower, and the resulting artistic effort is often a tulip. Children cannot resist them; I fell under their spell at the age of five and never recovered. Is it any wonder that they would fuel the fires of Tulipomania in seventeenth-century Holland, nearly ruining the country's economy in outrageous, speculative buying of tulip futures? Actually, I do wonder why a grown man would trade (as in one documented case) two loads of wheat, four loads of rye, four oxen, eight pigs, twelve sheep, two casks of wine, four barrels of beer, two barrels of butter, a thousand pounds of cheese, a bed, a suit, and a silver tankard for a single bulb.

Perhaps the mystique of the tulip stems from its exotic origin. Species mainly inhabit mountainous areas and hillsides from western and central Asia. The palace gardens of the sultans of the Ottoman Empire were resplendent with tulips. They were introduced to Western cultivation in 1554 by Flemish peace emissary Ogier Ghiselin de Busbecq, who had been sent by Austrian Emperor Ferdinand I to seek an end to the siege of Vienna by Sultan Suleiman. De Busbecq not only accomplished his mission, but brought back bulbs that resembled a turban (in Persian *toliban*, although he heard it as *tulipam*.) In time, the name of the new status symbol was shortened to tulip, the bulbs circulated among aristocratic Europeans, and the madness was on.

What the Dutch prized most dearly were the streaked varieties—so prominent in the masters' still-life paintings of the era—that were, in fact, caused by a virus. The virus "broke" solid-colored tulips into fantastic, feathered wonders. The Dutch had no knowledge of viruses and germs, so any tulip might "break" to wondrous results and profits. They fell for it—hook, line, and sinker—and the resulting wheeling and dealing in tulip futures and the eventual collapse, make modern stock market gyrations look like small potatoes in comparison. From the ashes of Tulipomania, however, rose the phoenix of the Dutch bulb industry.

Tulipomania lives, albeit on a smaller scale, each fall, when gardeners throw caution to the wind and order more tulips than they know what to with. I suspect that, as in my case, the first introduction of many gardeners to growing bulbs in containers comes from ordering too many tulips. It is easier on the back to pot them up than to plant the bulbs in the ground.

Some varieties of tulips grow more successfully in pots than others. Catalogues and garden

A WOODEN CRATE BRIMS WITH THE CLASSIC DARWIN TULIP, 'GOLDEN APELDOORN', *left*. THE TRIUMPH VARIETY 'APRICOT BEAUTY', *above*, IS FAVORED FOR ITS LOVELY COLOR AND DEPENDABILITY.

centers often label them "good for forcing." There are so many cultivated tulips—perhaps thousands—that like *Narcissus*, they are divided into classes—in this case by their flowering time and flower shape, to keep them straight.

Any tulip with a Christmas name, such as 'Jingle Bells', are especially bred for very early blooming for the holidays. Single early tulips, such as orange and purple 'Princess Irene', grow reliably in pots. Double early tulips including 'Peach Blossom' also perform well. Early Kaufmanniana tulips include 'Waterlily' and my favorite, 'Shakespeare'.

Among the midseason flowering tulips, the Darwin hybrids, such as red 'Apeldoorn', pale yellow 'Jewel of Spring', rose 'Elizabeth Arden', and 'Pink Impression', are almost fool-proof. Tall and graceful, they "twist and shout" as the blossoms open, the stems seemingly in a slow-motion dance. Greigii types such as 'Red Riding Hood' make excellent midseason bloomers as well.

The uniquely-colored Triumph tulip 'Apricot Beauty' may take the crown for beauty and dependability. Triumph tulips take longer to chill than most other tulips, and should be kept dark and cold until the middle of February.

The late flowering tulips include tall Darwin tulips, such as 'Golden Age', lily-flowered tulips, such as violet 'Maytime', bizarre parrot tulips, the Rembrandt tulips (the "broken" tulips of Tulipomania), and double late tulips, such as pink 'Angelique' and 'Gold Medal'.

In truth, almost any variety of tulip can succeed in a pot, providing that temperatures drop low enough (at least 40° F.) during its winter chill, the length of chilling is sufficient, fertilization is liberal, and that the sprouting bulbs are not hurried along too quickly with high temperatures. Their roots must be kept cool and moist.

Especially interesting are the small, showy species tulips. Yellow and white *Tulipa tarda* of Turkestan produces multiple blooms on stems just a few inches tall, while red *T. linifolia*, native to Bokhara in Asia, displays its brilliant flowers above thin, undulating leaves. *T. batalinii*, also from Bokhara, is especially attractive; its gray leaves complement its delicate apricot-colored blossoms.

Conventional wisdom has held that these true wild flowers could not be "forced" successfully. Nothing could be further from the truth; they are among the most fascinating denizens of spring.

T. BATALINII 'APRICOT JEWEL' STRETCHES GRACEFULLY.

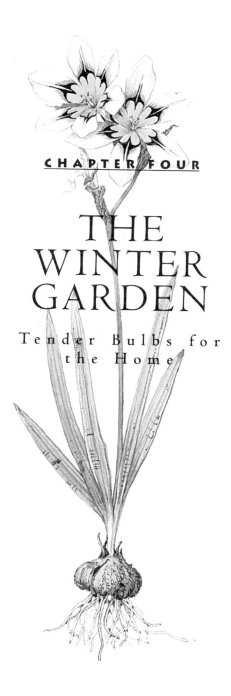

CHAPTER FOUR

THE
WINTER
GARDEN

Tender Bulbs for
the Home

Just as important on the windowsill as the flowers of spring are the tender beauties of the tropics and subtropics. Discontent need not be the watchword of winter. The outdoor garden is dormant, no doubt, but the windowsill is alive with a multitude of exotic flowers from bulbs.

Tender bulbs from around the world flower in the house during the winter or early spring with little specialized treatment. They often originate in tropical, subtropical, or maritime climates, and so adapt readily to life indoors. Many gardeners consider them seasonal houseplants.

The largest group of these bulbs are from the southern hemisphere. These plants from down under—especially Africa—bloom in our winter windows at the same time their kin often ride out the dry summer of their native habitat in a state of dormancy. *Clivia*, *Veltheimia*, and white calla lilies (*Zantedeschia aethiopica*) flower indoors in response to watering in the northern hemisphere just as their counterparts in South Africa bloom to the renewed moisture of the rainy season. Amaryllis (*Hippeastrum*) and gloxinia (*Sinningia*) from South America, respond to the warmth of our homes that simulate their natural environment.

FEW PLANTS ARE BETTER SUITED FOR INDOOR CULTURE THAN SOUTH AMERICAN AMARYLLIS.

THE SOUTH AFRICANS

By far the greatest number of tender, winter-flowering bulbs originate in South Africa. This is no surprise, considering the unique climate of that country and its incredible floral diversity. Approximately 10 percent of the world's species of plants are found in South Africa.

Bordered by the Indian Ocean on the east and the Atlantic on the west, the country enjoys two distinct climates, as well as a number of unusual microclimates. An imaginary line, drawn roughly down the center of the country, separates the two main climates and their flora. On the eastern side, summer monsoon moisture is followed by a mild, dry winter. In the west, the reverse is true: winters are rainy and summer dry. Furthermore, the western coast, particularly the Cape peninsula, receives the cold currents of the Antarctic.

To grow bulbs from the two areas successfully requires duplicating the conditions of their homelands. The eastern bulbs, including *Crocosmia*, *Gladiolus*, and *Nerine*, are best grown outdoors in summer in the United States. Originating in a specialized ecosystem of broadleaf evergreen forests in the Natal province, *Clivia* is the exception to the rule. It makes a superb indoor houseplant with showy winter blossoms.

The bulbous plants from the area around the Cape of Good Hope thrive indoors in winter across much of the continental U.S. *Albuca, Freesia, Lachenalia, Veltheimia,* and white *Zantedeschia,* prefer cool and moist growing conditions to flower, conditions easily provided indoors from November to February in temperate climates, and actually initiate bud growth in response to shorter days. As summer approaches, reduce watering and let them go partly or completely dormant.

The bulbs from the east coast above the Cape respond in much the same way, except that their summer is hot and bone-dry. *Babiana, Homeria, Ixia, Sparaxis,* and *Tritonia,* flower best, once again, under relatively cool conditions. They go completely dormant during summer and actually appreciate a good hot baking. They are often left in their pots by gardeners and stored in the garden shed, garage, or under the greenhouse bench for this summer treatment.

The east coast bulbs of South Africa make themselves quite at home in some mild parts of this country, especially California; the Bay area climate suits them especially well. For the rest of us, it is a question of simulating conditions for their culture as best we can. No one method works exactly the same for every gardener, and it is the experimentation, occasional failure, and ultimate triumph that makes growing them so rewarding.

TENDER MERCIES

The marketplace often dictates what bulbs can be procured for winter growing. This is often unfortunate, for bulbs are often offered by overseas growers at the wrong time for much of the country. *Ixia,* florist's anemones (*Anemone coronaria*), *Ranunculus,* and a host of others, particularly from South Africa, are often sold in spring. Since they are tender bulbs—not hardy in most of North America—some nurserymen assume that they should be treated as annuals. The trouble is that these bulbs are as sensitive to heat as they are to cold and many respond to day length to grow and set bud. They prefer relatively cool conditions and those that bloom in winter in their homelands set their clock by the short daylight hours of our winter. It is difficult to store these bulbs from the spring, when they are widely available, so that they can be used for winter flowering. The best way for us to enjoy these tender bulbs is indoors in the winter.

Gardeners with very bright conditions can enjoy winter pot culture with the bulbs that elsewhere bloom in the summer garden. In temperate climes, bulbs that require high light and long days to bloom well are best left for summer growing. But southern gardeners often split the difference, starting the bulbs indoors and flowering them outdoors during spring.

SINNINGIA, *above*, **AND** RANUNCULUS, *below*,

ENLIVEN WINTER WITH SPLASHES OF COLOR.

AUTUMN PLANTING

The time to plant tender, winter-flowering bulbs for indoor culture is in late summer through early winter. Potting is simple. Most true bulbs are planted with their necks at the soil surface, and corms and tubers such as *Sinningia* are planted just at or below the soil surface, depending on the species. Most other corms should be planted with an inch of soil over them, although *Freesia* benefit from being buried five inches deep.

A container must provide good drainage and enough room for the roots. A pot that is too big is like a pair of oversized galoshes: it is inefficient. The soil near the top and around the bulb dries up quickly, but becomes water-logged below. As with other bulbs, sharply drained soil—soil with generous amounts of sand, perlite, or vermiculite—is essential to tender bulbs.

Most, but not all, tender bulbs benefit from a cool rooting period before they grow and bloom; otherwise the bulbs will sprint into growth before they have a root structure to support what goes on above. (A few corms and tubers, including *Freesia* and *Ixia* provide the exception to the rule, rooting better under warm conditions.) For most of them, this mild chilling is easily accomplished once they have been potted. A few weeks in a cool, dark place, about 50° F., will suffice.

THE HOME FRONT

Each gardener must evaluate the conditions around his or her home to determine which tender bulbs can be grown and where. We can control indoors what we must leave to chance in the garden. Temperature and humidity may be manipulated to an extent, but keep in mind that tender bulbs differ in their needs. A cyclamen needs it cool, while Amazon lily prefers a jungle-like environment. Coexistence is nearly impossible—at least in the same room.

Light is a critical factor. There are only so many windows to go around. A west- or south-facing window is a boon to the bulb grower, but windows with other outlooks come in handy for some plants with lower light requirements, such as *Clivia*, *Cyclamen*, and *Veltheimia*. Artificial lights are useful to supplement the pale winter sun, especially in parts of the country with especially cloudy weather.

Generally, humidity is not as important a factor with bulbs as it is with houseplants such as ferns. The leaves of bulbous plants tend to be thick and fleshy, making them more tolerant to low humidity. Even so humidity levels in our homes drop drastically in the winter. Furnaces can blast living tissue dry, be it pine needles on the Christmas tree or human skin. Bulb foliage is not immune.

A humidifier effectively raises humidity around plants, but some of us are reluctant to live in a state of permanent dampness. The simple procedure of grouping plants together and adding pebbles to pot saucers is a time-honored way to increase humidity. Excess water accumulates in the gravel below the pot—which stays high and dry—and evaporates continually. This helps to prevent brown tips on the leaves and attacks by spider mites. Plants that need the most humidity, such as *Ranunculus* and florist's anemones, thrive in a cool bathroom, especially if the gardener is prone to long, steamy soaks in the tub. They also prosper on the kitchen windowsill above the sink, unless the automatic dishwasher has taken over dish duty.

HIGH TEMPERATURES AND HUMIDITY SUIT THE NEEDS OF
AMAZON LILY, EUCHARIS GRANDIFLORA.

AFTERCARE

Container-grown bulbs require what all plants do—a period of rest and a replenishment of resources. Evergreen plants, such as *Clivia*, show little sign of resting, but after flowering, they can stand a reduction in watering and fertilization: they are "on hold." They may stay in the same pot for years, so yearly top-dressing is necessary in the fall.

Evergreen bulbs and those that ripen their foliage late in the summer often join pots on the balcony or patio for a summer vacation. Care must be taken not to overexpose their leaves with the punishing rays of the sun, for it's not only the gardener who is susceptible to sunburn.

Other tender bulbs go completely dormant after their foliage ripens in spring or summer. They, too, are resting. In most cases, their pots are allowed to go, by degrees, completely dry. Some gardeners turn them on their sides to remind themselves not to water.

The bulbs may be dug and stored in a cool, dark place, but that's a lot of bother. It is much easier to remember a pot of resting bulbs when it comes time to revive them, than to remember a bag of bulbs stashed in the basement. If I find the bag at all, rummaging through the holiday decorations, old records, and bell-bottoms that I'm saving (just in case), I usually find that I did not label the bulbs in the first place. On the other hand, many gardeners possess organizational skills and memories far superior to mine.

ALBUCA

SENTRY-IN-A-BOX

The incredibly diverse flora of South Africa includes the relatively unknown genus *Albuca*, some thirty species strong, but only a few are in cultivation. The name *Albuca* comes from the Latin *albucus*, a name once given to asphodels. The flowers of some species of *Asphodel* are white; in other words, *albuca* means white. Talk about beating around the bush.

Nothing is going to get any clearer when discussing *A. canadensis*. It is definitely not from Canada—it grows wild near the Cape of Good Hope. A mixed-up French botanist in the seventeenth century included the plant in a book on Canadian plants, and we've had to live with his error ever since. The common name is not much more helpful; it takes a vivid imagination to find the pale sentry posted in the box of petals.

A. canadensis sports butter-yellow flowers tinged with olive, and a green stripe on each petal. The thin leaves, which grow up to several feet long, form a sinuous framework for the flower stalks.

It is easy to grow but it is hard to anticipate where in the house it will wind up, for it varies greatly in size; the flower stalks may grow anywhere from a foot and a half to three feet tall. The nodding flowers appear in early spring.

The bulbs, two inches in diameter, should be planted in fall in fertile, sharply drained soil with the tops of the bulbs just above the soil line. Albucas are grown cool—from 45° to 50° F. at night—and the soil should remain moist but not soggy. Cool sunrooms and window gardens suit the plants well. After the blossoms have faded, the basal foliage should be grown on as long as possible; when it has withered the pots stay dry until fall. The bulbs may be left in their pot until they become overcrowded.

Other species that lend themselves to pot culture are diminutive *A. humilis*, eight inches tall with white flowers striped green, and towering *A. nelsonii*, bearing striking white flowers with red stripes on five-foot stems.

A POT OF IVY MAKES A SPLENDID COMPANION FOR ALBUCA CANADENSIS.

ALLIUM

DAFFODIL GARLIC

THE COOL SUNROOM AT WAVE HILL IS PERFECT TO GROW A POT OF THREE-CORNERED LEEK, ALLIUM TRIQUETRUM, **WHICH RESPONDS BY BLOOMING FOR MONTHS IN WINTER.**

Onions are at the center of a controversy in the scientific community. Botanists are divided as to the family in which to place them: *Liliaceae*, *Amaryllidaceae*, or their own, *Alliaceae*. This has little bearing, however, on gardeners, who are more concerned about how the plants smell. In truth, many of the ornamental species bear sweet-scented flowers, and the leaves smell of onions only when cut or bruised.

Tender alliums are seldom grown in pots (except perhaps for the occasional pot of chives on the winter windowsill), but they have much to recommend them for pot culture. Among the best candidates is the onion of Naples, *A. neapolitanum*, sometimes known as the daffodil garlic; its pure white umbels of flowers on two-foot stalks make a pretty winter adornment.

European *A. triquetrum*, called three-cornered leek, carries graceful umbels of pendulous, green-striped, white flowers on unique, three-sided, eighteen-inch stems. The lavender-pink flowers of *A. perdulce* are borne on twelve-inch stems. All three are easily grown indoors in a cool position—from 45° to 50° F. at night—in bright light without a formal cold treatment. Potted in early fall, their bulbs just below the soil surface, they usually bloom in March.

The baboons of South Africa dig the corms of *Babiana* for food; Dutch settlers noticed this and followed suit during hard times. One dull winter's day, my friend Tom decided to try the experiment for himself. He ate a couple of corms and reports that they have a nutty taste, which he prefers to raw potatoes, and that they may have even greater potential dipped in chocolate. The plant's name is derived from the Dutch word for baboon, *babiaantje*.

The arching flower stems of baboon root rise above pleated, hairy leaves. Bright, six-petaled blossoms command attention. Only two of the thirty species of the genus are often grown. The deep purple, cupped flowers of *B. pulchra* that shade to red in the centers make pretty, ten-inch-tall pot specimens. Variable by nature, *B. stricta*, which has been cultivated since the beginning of the eighteenth century, has yielded a number of named varieties in white, crimson, lavender, and violet. Its flowering stems grow as tall as eighteen inches, and the flowers open wide into a star shape.

These tender babianas thrive in a pot with well-drained soil placed in bright, cool window. The soil should remain moist during the growing season and then allowed to go dry.

BABIANA

BABOON ROOT

THE PLEATED LEAVES OF BABIANA PULCHRA **ENHANCE ITS SHOWY, COLORED BLOSSOMS. IN SUMMER THE FOLIAGE WITHERS, WATER IS WITH-HELD AND THE POT IS STORED IN A DRY SPOT.**

BLETILLA

CHINESE GROUND ORCHID

Few bulbous plants possess the delicate beauty of *Bletilla striata*. Indigenous to the Orient, Chinese ground orchid differs from many of its tree-perched cousins by growing at ground level and by producing tuberlike bulbs.

The primly erect stems carry a few pleated leaves and grow from ten inches to almost two feet in height. They are topped by slightly nodding, lavender-pink blossoms up to two inches across. The lips are darker than the petals and dark purple ridges mark their middle lobes. A pure white-flowering form of *B. striata*, with a hint of pale yellow on the lip, is equally beautiful.

The cultivation of Chinese ground orchid is amazingly easy. The small bulbs revel in course, porous soil enriched with organic matter and are usually planted in autumn. Kept cool—at about 50° F. at night—and only slightly moist, the pot will be filled by new shoots in late winter when watering and fertilization is increased. After the flowers have faded, the foliage may be grown on inside or outdoors if it is protected from scorching sun. The leaves wither naturally in the fall and the bulbs rest until the cycle is repeated.

DECEPTIVELY DELICATE-LOOKING, CHINESE GROUND ORCHID IS EASY TO GROW IN A COOL, BRIGHT PORCH OR GREENHOUSE, *above*. CLIMBING ONION, *right*, SPREADS SPIDERY BRANCHES IN WINTER BUT NEEDS A SUMMER REST WHEN WATERING IS MINIMIZED.

BOWIEA

CLIMBING ONION

Of all the strange plants on the window-sill, few are as odd as the climbing onion, *Bowiea volubilis*. In its native habitat of Zambia, Zimbabwe, and South Africa, the thin, branched stems twine through other plants for support. Its round, green bulbs sit on the soil surface. Native Africans use them for a number of medical treatments, from headaches to infertility. *Bowiea*, named for nineteenth-century plant collector for Kew Gardens, J. Bowie, sometimes goes by the name Zulu potato.

Stems may reach as long as fifteen feet and bear tiny greenish white flowers on the tips. The fascination is with the bulbs themselves and the weaving branches, either climbing on neighboring house plants or trellises of bamboo or brush. Climbing onion needs bright indirect light or some sunshine.

WELL-ESTABLISHED CLIVIA BRIGHTEN A WINTER DAY AT LOGEE'S GREENHOUSES.

CLIVIA

NATAL LILY

A resurgence in all things Victorian may just usher *Clivia* back into the parlor. There is not a finer, care-free houseplant; its bright flowers are guaranteed to dismiss winter doldrums. The genus honors the Duchess of Northumberland, whose maiden name was Clive. If we are to remember the person for who a plant was named, as we must assume was intended, *Clivia* should definitely be pronounced with a long first "i."

The longstanding common name, kaffir lily, was an unfortunate choice, for kaffir is a derogatory term for native peoples of southern Africa. "Natal lily" has come into currency and become an often-used and more appropriate alternative, since the most common species, *C. miniata*, is indigenous to the Natal region.

Natal lily grows in broadleaf evergreen forests, and the region's winters are damp. Little wonder that it thrives in dim light indoors, and is among the most tolerant of bulbs to over-watering. Plants may eventually fill large containers with their leathery, deep green leaves. The striking umbels of wintertime flowers, however, are the real attraction. It is difficult to miss the brilliant orange, bell-shaped blossoms. They are carried in rounded clusters on strong, two-foot stems.

Blessed with an iron-clad constitution, *C. miniata* thrives with minimal care. Plants bloom best when crowded, although they have been known to "bust out" of confinement, sometimes rooting in greenhouse floors. Regular feeding in the fall encourages winter flower production, although the plants are known for surprise blooming out of season. Too dark of a position will inhibit flowering. Natal lily tolerates drafts and chills—even as low as 40° F.—without ill effect. No wonder it seems so at home in my century-old Victorian house.

A pretty yellow form 'Aurea' remains somewhat rare, but is increasingly coveted by devotees. The renewed interest in the species has resulted in breeding programs that will likely yield color and flower variations. A form with variegated leaves is highly prized.

C. nobilis is often overlooked, although it is also a superior year-round pot plant. Its flowers are borne in thick clusters of up to fifty or more on leafless stems growing to two feet or more. The pendant vermilion blossoms shade to apple-green at the mouth.

Both species of *Clivia* may be summered on a shady deck or under trees, where their dark foliage is always an asset.

Cyclamen

~

ALPINE VIOLET

COMELY CYCLAMENS, WITH THEIR UPSWEPT
PETALS AND HANDSOME SILVER-MARBLED
LEAVES, WILL LAST FOR MONTHS IF THEY ARE
KEPT COOL IN BRIGHT CONDITIONS.

Nothing brightens the winter window-sill like a pot of sprightly cyclamens, sometimes called alpine violets. The flowers hover like butterflies over the heart-shaped rosettes of leaves. Deep green and marbled with silver, they are worth growing for their own sake.

Like shades of nail polish, the translucent colors of cyclamens include pink, cherry red, magenta, cerise, and white. The breeders' triumph, all showy winter cyclamens were developed from a single species, *Cyclamen persicum*, from the eastern Mediterranean region. The name is handed down from the ancient Greeks.

Some, but not all, plants bear sweet, rose-scented flowers. Flower stems may reach ten inches in height, although miniature varieties only a few inches high pack as big of a floral wallop.

Planted indoors in autumn, the corms of cyclamens develop and bloom quickly, thriving in moisture-retentive soil under cool conditions. They are equally at home in a north or east window—close to the glass—or under lights.

I dutifully shuttle plants back to my chilly back porch each evening to keep them fresh. After a period in the limelight, tired plants get a shot of fertilizer and rejuvenate under lights. Corms go dormant as summer arrives; water is withheld while they rest until fall.

CYRTANTHUS

FIRE LILY

Perhaps a general disfavor of orange in interior design has hurt the popularity of flowers of that color. That's a shame, for the flowers of fire lily burn all the brighter contrasted by winter's ice. Although the common name aptly describes the yellow, orange, or red flowers, the name was first bestowed to the plant for the ability of the bulbs to survive and bloom after veld fires in South Africa. The scientific name means "curved flower" in Greek and describes the tubular blossoms.

Over forty species of fire lily occur in Africa, but few are cultivated in America. Clusters of up to twenty downward curving flowers, two or three inches long, top hollow stems above narrow, grassy leaves. *C. parviflorus* and *C. o'brienii* are noted for scarlet flowers. *C. mackenii*, has ivory, yellow, or apricot-pink flowers. The blossoms of evergreen *C. obliquus* shade from yellow at the base to orange, and finally to green at the tips.

The bulbs are planted just beneath the soil surface in deep pots to accommodate their delving roots. Well-drained soil, bright light, and cool winter temperatures—from 50° to 55° F. at night—suit fire lilies. Evergreen species are kept watered throughout the year, while others signal the need for a resting period by their yellowing foliage in summer.

DESPITE THEIR NAME, FIRE LILIES, *above,* **THRIVE IN COOL CONDITIONS. POTS OF AMAZON LILIES,** *right,* **FLOURISH IN A CONSERVATORY.**

EUCHARIS

AMAZON LILY

The Colombian Andes are home to lovely *Eucharis grandiflora*, treasured for its dramatic perfumed flowers. The slightly pendant, so-called Amazon lilies are carried on two-foot-tall stems. The well-chosen name *Eucharis* means "very graceful" in Greek.

Broad, shiny leaves set off the white blossoms, which measure as much as four inches across. Six petals surround a crown-shaped cup. Pale green in the interior, the cup is unusual in that the pollen-bearing anthers are poised on its points. A sniff of the flowers often results in a "powdered" nose.

Amazon lily prospers in a warm, humid environment with indirect light. Temperatures must not be allowed to fall below 65° F. at night. Humus-rich soil and moisture throughout the year are also necessary. A summer crop of flowers is sometimes produced after a low-water spring rest. Planted just deep enough to anchor them, the bulbs should remain undisturbed, spaced closely together in large, deep pots.

FREESIA

FRAGRANT FREESIA **AND MUSKY** MUSCARI **SHARE TEMPORARY QUARTERS WITH TRAILING IVY; A HUMID BUT WELL-VENTILATED ROOM KEEPS THE BLOSSOMS FROM FADING PREMATURELY.** GLADIOLUS TRISTUS **BLOOMS IN WINTER,** *right.*

A single, arched stem of *Freesia* perfumes an entire room with a clean sweetness that is never oppressive. Today's varieties, for convenience called *F. x hybrida*, bloom in lavender, purple, orange, rose-red, pink, yellow, and white, as well as double forms. Several of the eleven wild species from South Africa figure in their parentage. White-flowered hybrids, oddly enough, sometimes smell of ground black pepper. It is estimated that five percent of all people cannot smell freesias at all, even though they can smell other scented flowers. The genus name honors Friedrich Freese, a nineteenth-century German botanist.

Bringing *Freesia* into flower presents a challenge. Conventional wisdom mandates that the September-potted corms be grown in cool temperatures—50° F. at night—until the buds show, at which time the minimum night temperature is increased to 70° F. Based on my personal experience and that of professional growers, however, the reverse is better: warm first to promote good leaf growth, then cool to keep the buds from shriveling before they open. Gritty soil, relatively high humidity, and bright light are ideal. The corms do best planted with four or five inches of soil above them. Gardeners with greenhouses often succeed best.

GLADIOLUS

EVENING-SCENTED GLADIOLUS

Showy *Gladiolus* hybrids dominate the marketplace. Few gardeners get the opportunity to grow any of the exciting, unusual species, nor do we ordinarily give them a thought in winter. Although it can be grown outdoors, where it blooms late in the summer, *G. tristus* from the marshy flats of Cape Province in South Africa is highly prized for indoor winter pot culture.

Its graceful, winsome flowers—up to fifteen to a stem—bloom sulphur-yellow with pale green and brown markings. Its delicious fragrance, strongest after dark and on cloudy days, earned it the popular name of the night-scented gladiolus. It is sheer speculation on my part that a sensitive, poetic botanist chose the epitaph *tristus* for personal reasons; it means "sad." The hybrid 'Christabel' bears golden-yellow flowers with attractive russet stripes.

Flower spikes reach as high as forty inches (especially when they stretch during winter's low light) and usually need a ring of stakes and string to keep them from flopping. Even so girdled, the plants have an airy grace. Porous soil and weak but frequent applications of fertilizer ensure a prize-worthy pot.

GLORIOSA

GLORY LILY

A SUNNY BAY WINDOW TEEMS WITH TROPICAL TREASURES—FLAMING GLORIOSA LILIES FROM AFRICA AND INDIA, ALSTROEMERIA HYBRIDS FROM SOUTH AMERICA, AND SPOTTED CALLA LILIES FROM SOUTH AFRICA.

The brilliant, reflexed flowers of *Gloriosa* have thrilled Western admirers for more than four hundred years. Found in Africa and India, it bears the uncontestable name "full of glory." Some authorities regard all species as one variable one, *G. superba*, assigning differences to its wide geographic range. Gardeners and nurserymen, however, are reluctant to part with the name *G. rothschildiana*, honoring as it does the famous banking and gardening family.

Fingerlike tubers, planted horizontally just below the soil surface, sprout in midwinter from the pink "eyes." Fibrous, sandy soil promotes good growth. The thin stems climb with help from twining tendrils to six feet or more. The six reflexed yellow and red petals give the impression of a burst of flame.

The stems may be trained on a hoop or trellis for support. Moderately warm temperatures, 60° F. at night, and bright conditions suit glory lilies. While they may be moved outdoors to continue blooming into the summer, planting them in the ground is risky because they are all but irresistable to slugs. My friend Angela grows superb specimens in her kitchen with illumination from a skylight, as well as in her sun-drenched living room.

Does anyone really call this flower *Hippeastrum*? To flower lovers they are, and will always remain, amaryllis. Amaryllis blossoms, with their size and brilliance, cannot be ignored. They are often novice gardeners' introduction to indoor bulbs, and they are grown by the millions in winter windows.

The Victorians were in the throes of orchid-mania and interest in other exotica when amaryllis were first introduced from South America. The relatively small, funnel-shaped flowers of the original species were largely ignored at first.

Breeders took a hand in redesigning the genus and have achieved enormous flower heads painted in vibrant reds, oranges, pinks, and whites, often striped or shaded, or with picotee edging. Ironically, it is today's miniature varieties—akin to the original species—that have become wildly popular. 'Scarlet Baby' was one of the first, and has been followed by new, smaller, funnel shape flowered varieties in pink, white, and yellow. They offer the advantages of multiple stems of flowers in bloom at once, without the risky top-heavy flower heads.

The spectacle of the large hybrids, however, is still remarkable. Sophisticated gardeners sometimes frown on their floral extravagance, preferring a flower a bit more understated. That's too bad; does appreciating the artistry of the ballet preclude enjoying the spectacle of the circus? Colossal flower heads balance on hollow stems rising to as much as two feet. The plants need even moisture while in bloom to keep the vascular system from collapsing. The pots need to be turned a half turn each day to keep the stem from leaning towards the strongest light source. Even so, a big-headed beauty may take a nose-dive off the table without warning.

For this reason, a stiffer potting soil (with less perlite, sand, or vermiculite in the mix) and a deep clay pot help to anchor the bulb's roots. A stake or bulb ring is sometimes necessary, but this rather spoils the effect. Forsythia or cherry

HIPPEASTRUM

AMARYLLIS

FORSYTHIA BRANCHES OFFSET 'APPLE BLOSSOM' AMARYLLIS.

branches, stuck firmly into the soil, accomplish the chore more gracefully.

Bulbs may be potted anytime from September to May. The largest ones produce the most flowers on multiple spikes. I soak the roots and base of the bulb in tepid water overnight before planting. The upper half of the bulb should protrude above the soil. A tight fit is recommended for amaryllis, with only an inch or two of soil between the bulb and pot rim, but the pot must be deep enough to accommodate the roots. Bulbs are watered well after potting, but then sparingly until the nose of the bud emerges from the top of the bulb.

Timing is not exact, but given a daytime indoor temperature of 70° F., amaryllis will bloom in about six weeks. They may stall in a cooler environment, and it seems that each bulb keeps its own schedule, blooming when it is darned good and ready. Flowers last longer if kept away from furnace vents. Remove the flower stalks after the flowers fade, and they will usually be replaced by a second, and even a third. Some bulbs will produce two or more stems at once.

Leave the long, straplike leaves intact and encourage growth with frequent applications of all-purpose fertilizer. The object is to plump up the bulb for more flowers the next year. The time-honored tradition across the country has been to leave the pots on the porch or to summer them outdoors, bringing them indoors in early fall. By withholding water, the bulbs are induced to go dormant, rested for several months, and then coaxed to life again with water.

This does not work for everyone. Either the bulbs refuse to go dormant, or they fail to thrive, producing fewer flowers and declining in size. A new technique treats the growing bulbs like onions. They can be planted in the garden, carefully protecting the brittle leaves from sunburn and breakage for the first week. Fed regularly in rich loam, the bulbs increase in size over the summer. When the leaves are blackened by first frost, the bulbs are dug out, the foliage removed, and cured for a week in a cool, dry place indoors. After several months they can be repotted to start the spectacle all over. Southern gardeners often avoid the whole business by planting house-grown amaryllis in the garden after blooming, where they live and bloom with little care.

A TRIO OF 'SUSAN' AMARYLLIS ARE BACKED BY TALL 'HERCULES', EVEN TALLER 'APPLE BLOSSOM', AND FLOWERING QUINCE.

HOMERIA

CAPE TULIP

It is doubtful that Homer, the Greek poet, ever set eyes on the flowers that bear his name, since they are native to South Africa. First introduced to western horticulture late in the eighteen century, *Homeria collina* (also known as *H. breyniana*) is the best known of the forty-member genus, most of which are not in general cultivation.

Native to the Cape Peninsula, *H. collina* is known as Cape tulip for its six-petaled, cup-shaped flowers. Unlike its Dutch-bred namesake, however, cape tulips retain the charisma of wild flowers. Growing from a corm, with slender leaves as much as eighteen inches long, the two-inch diameter flowers are produced over several months. The blossoms of the variety 'Aurantiaca' glow in a shade of pale apricot, while 'Ochroleuca' is noted for honey-yellow flowers.

Cape tulip makes an excellent pot plant, although the wispy foliage may require an unobtrusive support, and a dozen or more tightly packed corms provide the best show. Homerias perform best in bright, cool conditions in moist, well-drained soil.

TINTED THE COLORS OF SHERBET, THE BLOSSOMS OF CAPE TULIP, *above*, BLOOM IN LATE SPRING INDOORS. POTS OF IXIA HYBRIDS, *below*, GRACE A DISPLAY AT THE PHILADELPHIA FLOWER SHOW.

IXIA

WAND FLOWER

Wand flowers wave as breezes rustle the grassy fields of the southwestern Cape of South Africa. The flexible, wiry stems—up to twenty inches tall—support tight clusters of six-petaled flowers, two inches across. They also go by the names corn lily and African bell. *Ixia* stems from the Greek *ixos*, meaning birdlime, and refers to the clammy sap of the plants. No attempt has been made, thank goodness, to call it the birdlime lily.

Breeders continue to produce colorful varieties exploiting some of the more than thirty distinct wild species of *Ixia*. Some of the species make pretty potted plants as well and are sometimes commercially available. The fiery orange flowers of *I. maculata* have a deep maroon center. Cultivated since the late eighteenth century, *I. viridiflora* still bewitches gardeners with its turquoise-green petals accented by a dark purple interior.

Wand flowers bloom above spearlike leaves in cool, bright conditions. The small corms flourish in well-drained soil and are allowed to dry out after the foliage withers. The flowers are extremely long-lasting, making them favorites for cutting, but the flowers open wide only in bright light.

WAND FLOWERS CLOSE AT NIGHT INTO TIGHT BELLS. RANUNCULUS **MAKE GOOD COMPANY FOR THEIR THIN LEAVES AND DISGUISE SPINDLY UNDERPINNINGS.**

LACHENALIA

LEOPARD LILY

South African gardeners call *Lachenalia*, found around the Cape of Good Hope, wild hyacinth or cape cowslip. Perhaps, however, the other common name, leopard lily, suits these exotic beauties best. The scientific name commemorates Werner de la Chenal, an eighteenth-century Swiss professor of botany.

L. aloides has been grown in Europe since before the American Revolution. It is such a variable species, however, that at least seven variations have at one time been considered as distinct species. (Bulbs labeled *pearsonii*, *quadricolor*, and *nelsonii* are all forms of *L. aloides*.) The pendant flowers shade from red to yellow to green, although the red fades with age.

Showy *L. bulbifera* (also called *L. pendula*) brightens the window with tomato-red flowers tipped with green or brown. Smaller-flowered but floriferous species include *L. glaucina*, called the opal lachenalia for the its color, and *L. arbothnotiae*, which blooms creamy white with a lavender-violet base.

The bulbs of *Lachenalia* are planted in fall, two inches deep, and spaced within several inches of each other to make a good show. The pots may be stored for the summer in a dry, dark spot after the plants go dormant.

LEDEBOURIA

SILVER SQUILL

The silver squills of Africa are close relatives of the *Scilla* of the northern hemisphere. The genus *Ledebouria*, named in honor of nineteenth-century Estonian botanist Karl Friedrich von Ledebour, differs from *Scilla* in having purple-mottled, often silvery, leaves and very little cold tolerance. They grace the greenhouse or window ledge in gardens where frost occurs.

Attractive even when not in bloom, *L. socialis* from South Africa needs no special care to put on a good show. *Socialis* denotes its habit of growing together in dense colonies. The arching leaves, up to five inches long and an inch wide, glint silver against the burgundy patches. Delicate spikes of long-lasting, greenish-white flowers complete the picture.

The bulbs of silver squill are buried up to their necks, closely-spaced, in small pots filled with porous soil. They are kept moist from fall through winter, and gradually dried out as the fading foliage signals the need to rest. In humid environs they may remain evergreen.

BRILLIANT RED-AND-YELLOW LACHENALIA ALOIDES **IS GROUPED WITH IVY, ALLIUM, AND OSTEOSPERMUM,** *left.* LACHENALIA ARBOTHNOTIAE, *above left*, **DISPLAYS THE OTHER END OF THE COLOR SPECTRUM. SILVER SQUILLS,** *above*, **RESEMBLE THEIR HARDY NORTHERN KIN BUT PREFER THE COMPANY OF TENDER CACTI AND SUCCULENTS.**

Christmas wouldn't be the same without paperwhites. Mingling with the scents of pine boughs and cinnamon, paperwhite's piercing sweetness is as essential to my holiday mood as carols and eggnog. Not everyone shares my rapture. I delivered a pot to my neighbors one holiday; they returned it the next day with the frank appraisal that the flowers smelled of dirty socks.

The scent of selected varieties and hybrids is milder. Creamy yellow 'Israel' carries a gentle musky fragrance, as do shorter, brighter 'Bethlehem' and 'Nazareth'. Pure white 'Galilee' and 'Jerusalem' possess a less potent scent than standard kinds. I will try again with my sensitive-nosed neighbors.

The flowers of 'Grand Soleil d'Or' are golden yellow with an orange cup, and those of 'Chinese Sacred Lily', whose name was a turn-of-the-century marketing ploy to give it a mysterious aura, are white with a saffron yellow cup. It is not a reliable bloomer and should be purchased from reputable merchants; much of the stock is said to be infected by virus.

Most home bulb fanciers first cut their teeth growing paperwhites—hybrids and varieties of tender *Narcissus tazetta* and *N. papyraceus*, both native to Portugal, Spain, and France, as well as several

Narcissus

PAPERWHITES

CUT FROM THE WINTER GARDEN, BERRIED
STEMS OF EUONYMUS SUPPORT PAPERWHITES
WITH STYLE, *left*. CRANBERRIES REPLACE
PEBBLES AT CHRISTMAS. *above*.

THE YEARLY RITE OF SEED ORDERING IS
A PLEASANT WINTER PASTIME ACCOMPANIED
BY PAPERWHITES, CYCLAMENS, VELTHEIMIA,
AND SCENTED GERANIUMS.

other species from the western Mediterranean region. They have been perfuming musty rooms for centuries. The bulbs grow readily in soil or in pebbles with water. If planted in pebbles, gravel, or sand, the bulbs are covered to their necks after the water level has been checked to see that it rises in the container only to their bases; higher levels can cause rot. Two to four weeks in a cool, dark closet or cupboard after planting allows the roots to develop.

An old trick to keep the flower stems from getting lanky is to add a teaspoon of gin to the water. I learned this from Brent Heath at the Daffodil Mart, who, in turn, got the tip from a gardener in New England. A biologist friend of mine was horrified when I told her I was going to try it—something about poisoning my plants—but I went ahead. In a completely unscientific test with side-by-side pots, I watered one with gin—one teaspoon to a quart of water—and one without. The gin-ladled plants did indeed stay shorter but flowering was uneven. I decided to reserve the gin for guests.

If my paperwhites get floppy, I tie them with a raffia bow or support them with berried branches from the garden. Rose hips, winter berry, and *Euonymus* berries turn an ordinary pot of paperwhites into a work of art.

PHAEDRANASSA

QUEEN LILY

Queen lily had its heyday in the Victorian era and has never recaptured the public's attention. The unusual name is derived from the Greek *phaidros*, gay, and *anassa*, queen. The Phaedra of mythology, however, was anything but a happy character. When her stepson, Hippolytus, rejected her love, she accused him of raping her. A sea monster sent by Poseidon frightened the horses pulling his chariot along the beach. He was thrown and dragged to his death; Phaedra hanged herself in despair.

Native to the Andes Mountains, the bulbs are found growing at lower elevations and are not hardy in gardens where frost occurs, but they thrive indoors in cool, sunny situations and may be grown much like amaryllis.

The tips of the vermilion red flowers of *P. carmioli* appear to have been dipped in a green paint pot. On mature bulbs, as many as a dozen pendant, two-inch-long flowers are clustered at the top of two-foot-tall stalks. The flowers of *P. chloracra* are similar except for their rosy purple color. The narrow leaves are frequently produced after the flowers and must be allowed to ripen before the pots are dried out and rested during the summer.

RARE BUT LOVELY; PHAEDRANASSA CARMIOLI **REACHES REGAL HEIGHTS.**

RANUNCULUS

PERSIAN BUTTERCUP

When a friend of mine was courting his wife-to-be, he always brought her brightly-colored Persian buttercups, which she held in far greater esteem than roses. Little did he know that he was following an ancient tradition. *Ranunculus asiaticus* from Asia Minor has long been in cultivation and was first grown in Europe at the end of the sixteenth century. The name is derived from *rana*—Greek for "frog"—because many species (few of them bulbous) grow in damp places.

All of the dazzling modern Persian buttercups have been selected from the single wild species over many centuries.

Flower stems rise as high as fifteen inches. Finely divided leaves spring from the claw-shaped tubers, which are usually soaked for a few hours before they are planted in sandy soil. Persian buttercups thrive in humid, cool conditions.

RANUNCULUS **ARE SOMETIMES CALLED FAIR-MAIDS-OF-FRANCE, PERHAPS BECAUSE THEY MIMIC THE SKIRTS OF CANCAN DANCERS.**

SINNINGIA

GLOXINIA

In no other flower, aside from amaryllis, is the hand of the breeder so evident. Gardeners consider the florist's gloxinia either an apparition or an abomination.

There is no denying the grandeur of these flowers. The texture is that of velvet, and the colors—especially the sumptuous reds and royal purples—are richer than the pigments on any painter's palette.

The modern race of hybrid *Sinningia* bears little resemblance to the wild tropical species of Central and South America. Named for the head gardener at the University of Bonn, Wilhelm Sinning (1794-1874), many of the species were introduced during the nineteenth century. Modern varieties descend primarily from a Brazilian species, *S. speciosa*, introduced in 1815.

A Belgian nurseryman, Louis Van Houtte, made a lasting impact in 1866 when he introduced a variety bearing bright carmine-red flowers with a white edge. He named it for his wife, Gloxinia.

The tubers of gloxinias are best started in the early spring for summer flowering, although they

A SATIN-TEXTURED GLOXINIA CONTRASTS
WITH HYACINTHS AND NARCISSUS,
above. SPARAXIS ELEGANS, *right,* **BLOOMS**
AT LONGWOOD GARDENS.

can be manipulated to bloom almost throughout the year. The tubers are pressed gently into the soil surface; a fine, humusy soil is advisable.

They require evenly moist conditions and warm temperatures, not falling below 60° F. at night, as one might expect from them knowing their tropical ancestry. Gloxinias are plants of the forest floor and should never be subjected to full sun, preferring, instead, bright, indirect light.

The thick, dark green leaves display the flowers to advantage. Despite their appearance, they are fragile and must be handled with care. Those that do break off, however, may be inserted into soil to root as is the common practice with African violets. Gloxinias grown from seed produce flower-sized plants in about six months.

First-time gloxinia growers panic when the plants begin to go dormant after flowering. They inevitably drown them in water and fertilizer, and end up consigning them to the garbage. Plants must be allowed to dry out gradually—although they should never be completely dry—and after a rest period of a month or more, the plant will show signs of new growth and watering can be increased. Gloxinias so treated may last for decades; it is not unheard of to find some as wide as a bushel basket.

SPARAXIS

HARLEQUIN FLOWER

The pattern of an open-faced *Sparaxis* flower is like a kaleidoscope. The yellow center is often outlined in black, surrounded by six petals of orange, white, yellow, or deep red. The nickname harlequin flower could not be more appropriate. The genus is indigenous to the Cape Province of South Africa and were first introduced in the late 1700s. The name is derived from the Greek *spares*, to tear. It refers to the bracts surrounding the flowers that appear to have been lacerated (a feature that few of us would notice as we gaze into the beautiful blossom).

Fan-shaped leaves support branched stems, a foot tall, topped by flowers opening as much as three inches wide. The species *S. tricolor* is most often grown, although two others merit attention. The variable *S. elegans* (formerly classified as *Streptanthera*) is noted for the varieties 'Zwanenburg' with maroon petals surrounding a yellow center, and 'Coccinea' with copper-orange petals highlighting a black center. Harlequin flowers should be treated much like *Babiana* or *Ixia*, and the corms may be left in the same pot for several years until they become overcrowded. Potted in autumn, they need several weeks to root and should be watered sparingly and kept cool.

TRITONIA

FLAME FREESIA

A CART, *above*, HOSTS A SUNROOM DISPLAY OF TRITONIA HYBRIDS. VELTHEIMIA BRACTEATA, *right*, WILL FORM A LARGE CLUMP.

South Africa is a horticultural treasure trove. Almost too many related plants have been mined from its unique flora, and many are overshadowed by more popular cousins. *Tritonia crocata* was first introduced in 1758 but has never been as widely grown as it deserves.

The name *Tritonia* is derived from the Greek *triton*, a weathercock, and refers to the flower stamens that change direction. This unusual feature is not as striking as the flowers themselves, whose six petals are translucent on either side of their base. These little center "windows" only add a fragile delicacy to the two-inch-wide, cup-shaped blossoms.

The orange and yellow flowers of *T. crocata* dot the grassy fields the southwestern Cape Province. The name flame freesia is a fitting one, and it is sometimes called blazing star. Selected forms bloom in shades of Italian ice: frosty peach, salmon, cream, and amber yellow. The foot-tall flower spikes, bearing up to a dozen buds, rise above a basal fan of sword-shaped leaves. The small corms of *Tritonia* are best started indoors in midwinter, and grow and bloom best before the onset of summer heat, and may be dried and stored in a cool, dry spot.

VELTHEIMIA

WINTER-RED-HOT-POKER

The Victorians grew veltheimias in great numbers. This is not surprising, since they make excellent container plants of good size, tolerate a variety of conditions, and bloom in the late winter and early spring. The name winter-red-hot-poker, while descriptive of the dense racemes of flowers, may lead to confusion with the unrelated genus *Kniphofia*, which is also called red hot-poker. Cape lily is often used, signifying the South African origins of the plants. The genus *Veltheimia* is named for an eighteenth century patron of botany, August Ferdinand Graf von Veltheim.

Only two species comprise the genus, although the two have several distinct forms. *V. capensis* is native to the Atlantic side of the Cape Province of South Africa, while *V. bracteata* grows on the Indian Ocean side. The Victorians, through selection, grew many more varieties with color and foliage differences. The resurgence of interest in growing these handsome plants may bring back a greater range of selections.

V. bracteata grows in coastal woodlands, so it thrives in bright light without direct sunshine. Rosettes of shiny, deep green leaves, wavy at the margins, set off flowering spikes of up to fifty blossoms on stems up to twenty inches high. The two-inch-long, tubular, drooping flowers are pale pink, brushed with mint-green at the tips.

V. capensis, found growing on dry hillsides, is distinguished by the bluish-green leaves, usually several inches shorter than *V. bracteata's* normal eighteen inches. The margins of the leaves are also wavy. The flowers, borne on sixteen-inch stems, are about half the size of the other species, but are richer in color.

Both species bloom in winter, between December and April indoors. I've noticed that *V. bracteata* on my back porch often initiates buds at Thanksgiving. The plants tolerate cool, damp conditions (down to 40° F.) and low light—perhaps the reason Victorians succeeded so well. It is interesting to speculate what led to the decline in their popularity. Was it the stiff, rather appearance of the flowers, or central heating?

Veltheimias are planted in well-drained soil in autumn, with an inch of soil covering the tops of the bulbs. They are kept moist during the growing season, with less moisture in the summer; *V. capensis* may go completely dormant, as it does in the wild, until the fall. Veltheimias eventually form impressive clumps in large containers. They may be summered outdoors in the shade. Adaptable and nearly carefree, these charmers are overdue for a comeback.

WATSONIA

BUGLE LILY

ZANTEDESCHIA

CALLA LILY

The flowers of *Watsonia* flare like its bugle namesake, and, in many respects, resemble slender, graceful gladiolus, to which it is closely related. The South African genus was named for the eighteenth-century English physician and naturalist Sir William Watson, whose passion was electrical experiments.

Watsonia is a large genus and contains species that range in height from one to five feet, with the shortest ones adapting best to pot culture. The flowers are held in a flat plane facing away from each other. The salmon pink flowers of *W. brevifolia* are held on sixteen-inch stems over short leaves. The faintly scented blossoms of *W. humilis* are mauve pink, and those of *W. coccinea* are scarlet. Selections and hybrids display peach, cream, white, or pink flowers. Bugle lilies are not demanding: pot in fall for spring flowers, water liberally, provide bright light, and let pots gradually go dry after blooming.

Vellum-textured spathes of calla lilies— almost more sculpture than flower—are held in high esteem everywhere except in its South African homeland. There, growing in every ditch, swamp, and creek bed, elegant *Z. aethiopica* is known as ditch lily or pig lily.

Several long flower stems may grace the handsome foliage clumps in late winter and spring. The tiny, overlooked yellow flowers that are encircled by the white spathe bear a soft, sweet scent. The green-stained spathe of the variety 'Green Goddess' is either a flower of unequaled beauty or merely bizarre, depending on one's point of view.

Thick rhizomes support plants growing as tall as six feet. They perform best in moist, nearly swampy soil. Since they cannot tolerate excessive summer heat, they make excellent container plants where space allows. The white calla lily is evergreen in frost free areas.

THE ZIG-ZAG BUDS OF A WATSONIA BREVIFOLIA **HYBRID**, *above left,* OPEN INTO FLARING BUGLES. ESTEEMED IN ALL BUT ITS HOMELAND, THE WHITE CALLA LILY OOZES ELEGANCE, *left.*

TIME TABLE FOR COLD TREATMENT OF SPRING-FLOWERING BULBS

(TIMING IS APPROXIMATE DEPENDING ON TEMPERATURES; 33–40° F. IS IDEAL UNLESS NOTED.)

ALLIUM
- MOLY .... 14–16 WEEKS
- OREOPHILUM .... 14–16 WEEKS
- KARATAVIENSE .... 18–22 WEEKS

ANEMONE
- BLANDA .... 8–10 WEEKS

BRODIAEA (AT 45° F.) .... 14–16 WEEKS

CAMASSIA .... 12–15 WEEKS

CHIONODOXA .... 10–14 WEEKS

CONVALLARIA .... 10–12 WEEKS

CROCUS .... 8–10 WEEKS

FRITILLARIA
- MELEAGRIS .... 10–12 WEEKS
- PERSICA .... 14–18 WEEKS

GALANTHUS .... 9–12 WEEKS

HYACINTHUS .... 12–15 WEEKS

IPHEION .... 12–14 WEEKS

IRIS
- DANFORDIAE .... 10–14 WEEKS
- RETICULATA .... 10–14 WEEKS
- HISTRIODES .... 10–14 WEEKS
- BUCHARICA .... 12–14 WEEKS
- DWARF BEARDED .... 14–16 WEEKS

LEUCOJUM
- VERNUM .... 10–12 WEEKS
- AESTIVUM .... 8–10 WEEKS

LILIUM
- ASIATIC HYBRIDS .... 12–16 WEEKS

MUSCARI .... 10–14 WEEKS

NARCISSUS .... 12–15 WEEKS

RHODOHYPOXIS (NEVER BELOW FREEZING) . 10–12 WEEKS

SCILLA
- SIBERICA .... 10–12 WEEKS
- TUBERGENIANA .... 10–12 WEEKS
- CAMPANULATA .... 12–14 WEEKS
- PRATENSIS (NEVER BELOW FREEZING) .... 8–10 WEEKS
- PERUVIANA (NEVER BELOW FREEZING) .... 8–12 WEEKS

TULIPA .... 12–16 WEEKS

SOURCES

B & D Lilies
330 P Street
Port Townsend, WA 98368 $1

Bakker of Holland
Louisiana, MO 63353
(spring bulbs)

Bundles of Bulbs
112 Green Springs Valley Road
Owings Mills, MD 21117
(wide selection)

The Daffodil Mart
Rt. 3, Box 794
Gloucester, VA 23061 $1
(wide selection of *Narcissus, Crocus,*
and *Tulips* as well as hard-to-find
*Allium, Brodiaea, Camassia, Fritillaria,
Iris, Ixia, Lachenalia*)

P. de Jager & Sons
P.O. Box 2010
South Hamilton, MA 01982
(wide selection)

Dutch Gardens
P.O. Box 200
Adelphia, NJ 07710
(wide selection)

Logee's Greenhouses
141 North Street
Danielson, CT 06239 $3
(exotic houseplants including
some bulbs)

McClure & Zimmerman
P.O. Box 368
108 W. Winnebago
Friesland, WI 53935
(wide selection including hard-to-
find species tulips, *Anemone, Freesia,
Fritillaria, Galanthus, Ipheion, Iris, Ixia,
Lachenalia, Leucojum, Scilla, Sparaxis,
Veltheimia, Watsonia*)

Messelaar Bulb Co.
P.O. Box 269
Ipswich, MA 01938
(wide selection)

Mitsch Daffodils
P.O. Box 218
Hubbard, OR 97032 $3

Mt. Hood Lilies
15361 SE Bluff Road
P.O. Box 1314
Sandy, Oregon 97055

Oregon Trail Daffodils
3207 SE Mannthey
Corbett, OR 97019

Park Seed Co.
Cokesbury Road
Greenwood, SC 29647-0001
(wide selection including *Babiana,
Bletilla, Bowiea*)

John Scheepers Inc.
P.O. Box 700
Bantam, CT 06750
(wide selection of spring bulbs)

Smith & Hawken
25 Corte Madera
Mill Valley, CA 94941
(specialty indoor bulbs and containers)

White Flower Farm
Litchfield, CT 06759-0050
(spring bulbs and some specialty
indoor bulbs including *Clivia,
Convallaria, Cyclamen, Freesia,
Zantedeschia*)

K. Van Bourgondien & Sons Inc.
P.O. Box 1000
245 Farmingdale Road, Rt. 109
Babylon, NY 11702-0598
(spring bulbs and tender indoor bulbs)

Van Engelen, Inc.
307 Maple Street
Litchfield, CT 06759
(wide selection of spring bloomers)

BIBLIOGRAPHY

Bryan, John E. *Bulbs*, Vol. I, II. Portland, OR: Timber Press, 1989.

Coombes, Allen J. *Dictionary of Plant Names*. Portland, OR: Timber Press, 1985.

Crockett, James Underwood. *Bulbs*. Alexandria, VA: Time-Life Books, 1971.

De Hertogh, August, Dr., *Holland Bulb Forcer's Guide*. Hillegom, The Netherlands: International Flower-Bulb Centre, 1989.

Elliot, Jack. *Growing Dwarf Bulbs (A Wisley Handbook)*. London: Cassell, 1988.

Everett, Thomas H., ed. *The New York Botanical Garden Illustrated Encyclopedia of Horticulture*. New York: Garland Publishing Inc., 1981.

Grey-Wilson, Christopher and Mathew, Brian. *Bulbs, The Bulbous Plants of Europe and Their Allies*. London: William Collins Sons & Co. Ltd, 1981.

Grimal, Pierre. *A Concise Dictionary of Classical Mythology*. Oxford: Basil Blackwell Ltd, 1990.

Lawrence, Elizabeth. *The Little Bulbs*. Durham: Duke University Press, 1986.

Martin, Tovah. *The Essence of Paradise*. Boston: Little, Brown, and Co., 1991.

————. *Once Upon a Windowsill*. Portland, OR: Timber Press, 1988.

Miles, Bebe. *The Wonderful World of Bulbs*. Princeton: D. Van Nostrand Company, Inc., 1963.

Peters, Ruth M. *Bulb Magic in Your Window*. New York: M. Barrows and Company, Inc., 1954.

Rix, Martin. *Growing Bulbs*. Beaverton, OR: Timber Press, 1983.

Schneider, Alfred F., *Park's Success with Bulbs*. Greenwood, SC: Geo. W. Park Seed Co., Inc., 1981.

Scott, George Harmon. *Bulbs, How to Select, Grow, and Enjoy*. Tucson, AZ: HP Books, Inc., 1982.

Mathew, Brian. *The Smaller Bulbs*. London: B.T. Batsford Ltd, 1987.

————. *The Year-Round Bulb Garden*. London: Souvenir Press Ltd, 1986.

INDEX

GIANT RANUNCULUS.